SIMPLIFYING
THE JOURNEY

SIX STEPS TO SCHOOLWIDE COLLABORATION, CONSISTENCY, AND CLARITY IN A PLC AT WORK®

Bob Sonju • Maren Powers • Sheline Miller

FOREWORD BY MIKE MATTOS

Solution Tree | Press

a division of
Solution Tree

555 North Morton Street
Bloomington, IN 47404
800.733.6786 (toll free) / 812.336.7700
FAX: 812.336.7790

email: info@SolutionTree.com
SolutionTree.com

Visit **go.SolutionTree.com/PLCbooks** to download the free reproducibles in this book.

Printed in the United States of America

Library of Congress Cataloging-in-Publication Data

Names: Sonju, Bob, 1967- author. | Powers, Maren, author. | Miller,
   Sheline, author.
Title: Simplifying the journey : six steps to schoolwide collaboration,
   consistency, and clarity in a PLC at work / Bob Sonju, Maren Powers,
   Sheline Miller.
Other titles: 6 steps to school wide collaboration, consistency, and
   clarity in a professional learning community at work
Description: Bloomington, IN : Solution Tree Press, [2023] | Includes
   bibliographical references and index.
Identifiers: LCCN 2023024242 (print) | LCCN 2023024243 (ebook) | ISBN
   9781958590072 (paperback) | ISBN 9781958590089 (ebook)
Subjects: LCSH: Professional learning communities--United States. |
   Teaching teams--United States.
Classification: LCC LB1731 .S58 2023 (print) | LCC LB1731 (ebook) | DDC
   371.100973--dc23/eng/20230831
LC record available at https://lccn.loc.gov/2023024242
LC ebook record available at https://lccn.loc.gov/2023024243

Solution Tree
Jeffrey C. Jones, CEO
Edmund M. Ackerman, President

Solution Tree Press
President and Publisher: Douglas M. Rife
Associate Publishers: Todd Brakke and Kendra Slayton
Editorial Director: Laurel Hecker
Art Director: Rian Anderson
Copy Chief: Jessi Finn
Senior Production Editor: Tonya Maddox Cupp
Text and Cover Designer: Julie Csizmadia
Acquisitions Editors: Carol Collins and Hilary Goff
Assistant Acquisitions Editor: Elijah Oates
Content Development Specialist: Amy Rubenstein
Associate Editor: Sarah Ludwig
Editorial Assistant: Anne Marie Watkins

Acknowledgments

The realization of this book is possible because of countless people who have inspired and taught me so much. To my coauthors and friends, Maren Powers and Sheline Miller, who are never satisfied with the status quo and always striving to be better. To Tonya Cupp, our editor and coach, for her extensive expertise and gentle nudging, which has allowed our collective thoughts to become words on a page. The term inspiration doesn't seem sufficient enough to describe Rick and Becky DuFour and Dr. Bob Eaker for their life's work and being compassionately relentless in improving learning for all students and educators. I'd also be remiss if I didn't thank my friend Mike Mattos for his inspiring passion for this work and always being willing to be a phone call away. Finally, to my wife, Leslye, and four beautiful daughters, Macey, Madi, Halle, and Andie, who embody everything that is good in the world.

I want to extend my deepest appreciation to educators everywhere for the profound impact you have on our world each day. With every lesson you teach, every challenge you help students overcome, and every word of encouragement you offer, you are a true inspiration; you are ambassadors of hope in a world that desperately needs you. Thank you for the extraordinary work you do each day.

—Bob Sonju

Being able to write this book with my coauthors and dear friends has been one of my greatest joys professionally. I'd like to dedicate my work to my husband, Darren, and our two boys. You three are the reason for everything. You all inspire me to be the best version of myself every day. Thank you. To my biggest cheerleaders: my family. For their constant encouragement and love. I could not have done any of this without all of you (and your babysitting). In particular, Grandma and Mom: thank you for showing me what hard-working and kind women look like. You both epitomize that. Finally, to the wonderful humans I have been lucky enough to call my teammates over the years: Amy, Katie, and Aymee. Your constant trust and willingness to change the way we do things in education were the spark that began this book. I love and thank you all.

—Maren Powers

This book is something I never in my wildest dreams thought was possible. Thank you to my coauthors, Bob Sonju (a great mentor) and Maren Powers (an awesome colleague who helped me grow and learn). These two people, combined with the amazing faculty and staff at Washington Fields Intermediate School, have inspired and pushed me to become better than I ever thought possible. I would be remiss not to dedicate this book to my two children, Talore and Colton, who followed in their mama's footsteps and became educators themselves. I hope this book can make their lives easier and increase their capacity to impact student learning. Lastly, thank you to my husband, oldest son, and mom for putting up with my self-doubt and craziness throughout the entire process. It really does take the collective skills and help of those around us to be successful. Thank you all!

—Sheline Miller

Solution Tree Press would like to thank the following reviewers:

Doug Crowley
Assistant Principal
DeForest Area High School
DeForest, Wisconsin

Jennifer Shaver
Principal
Deer Creek 4th & 5th Center
Edmond, Oklahoma

Sheryl Walters
Instructional Design Lead
Calgary, Alberta, Canada

Dianne Yee
Assistant Professor of Education
Western University
London, Ontario, Canada

Visit **go.SolutionTree.com/PLCbooks** to download the free reproducibles in this book.

Table of Contents

Reproducibles are in italics.

About the Authors ix

Foreword: The Unexpected Depth of Simplicity xi

by Mike Mattos

Introduction 1

The Action 3

Leading the Work—Specific Actions of School and Team Leaders 6

Coaching the Work—Specific Actions of Learning Coaches 7

Don't Miss This 9

Team Coaching Inventory 10

1 Identifying Essential Standards and Skills 13

Leading the Work—Specific Actions of School and Team Leaders 14

Coaching the Work—Specific Actions of Learning Coaches 17

Don't Miss This 27

Identifying the Essential Standards—Meeting Agenda 29

Identifying the Essential Standards and Skills Cards 32

Team Essential Standards Guide 33

Gaining Shared Clarity and Defining Mastery 35

Leading the Work—Specific Actions of School and Team Leaders . . . 36

Coaching the Work—Specific Actions of Learning Coaches 40

Don't Miss This 55

Gaining Shared Clarity—Meeting Agenda 56

Gaining Shared Clarity Cards 57

Teacher Team Workshop—Gaining Shared Clarity 58

Gaining Shared Clarity 61

Encouraging Student Ownership Through Student Self-Assessment 63

Leading the Work—Specific Actions of School and Team Leaders . . . 63

Coaching the Work—Specific Actions of Learning Coaches 65

Don't Miss This 83

Utilizing Formative Assessment for Feedback 87

Leading the Work—Specific Actions of School and Team Leaders . . . 88

Coaching the Work—Specific Actions of Learning Coaches 91

Don't Miss This 105

Targeted Unit Plan 106

Learning From Formative Data 115

Leading the Work—Specific Actions of School and Team Leaders . . . 117

Coaching the Work—Specific Actions of Learning Coaches 119

Don't Miss This 127

Creating Extra Time and Support for Learning 129

Leading the Work—Specific Actions of School and Team Leaders . . . 129

Coaching the Work—Specific Actions of Learning Coaches 132

Don't Miss This 141

Extra Time and Support Data Collection—Individual Teacher 142

Extra Time and Support Data Collection—Collaborative Team 144

Engaging in Focused, Productive Collaboration 147

Leading the Work—Specific Actions of School and Team Leaders . . . 148

Coaching the Work—Specific Actions of Learning Coaches 151

Don't Miss This 159

What We Collaborate About 160

Monitoring Collaboration 161

Weekly Team Meeting Agenda 162

Assessing Our Reality 163

Final Thoughts 167

References and Resources 169

Index 173

About the Authors

 **Bob Sonju** is an award-winning educational leader, author, and speaker nationally recognized for his energetic commitment to coaching educational leaders and teacher teams in research-based processes and systems that create the conditions for lasting success. Bob has led two separate schools to Model Professional Learning Community (PLC) at Work® status; one of his schools also received the prestigious National Breakthrough School Award from the National Association of Secondary School Principals. As a district leader, Bob led the implementation of the PLC process in a district composed of over fifty schools.

Bob was named Principal of the Year by the Utah Association of Secondary School Principals and was selected as one of three finalists for National Principal of the Year by the National Association of Secondary School Principals. His work has been published in the Solution Tree books *It's About Time: Planning Interventions and Extensions in Secondary School*; *Best Practices at Tier 2: Supplemental Interventions for Additional Student Support, Elementary*; *Help Your Team: Overcoming Common Collaborative Challenges in a PLC at Work*; and *Women Who Lead: Insights, Inspiration, and Guidance to Grow as an Educator*, as well as in the magazine *Principal Leadership*.

Bob earned a bachelor's degree, a master's degree, and an endorsement in school leadership from Southern Utah University.

Maren Powers is an award-winning educator and Solution Tree associate. She is a practicing language arts teacher and learning coach in the Washington County School District in Utah. Throughout her time in the district, Maren has worked and trained at two Model PLC schools: (1) Fossil Ridge Intermediate School and (2) Washington Fields Intermediate School. At Washington Fields, she was integral in the opening and implementation of the PLC process and school culture. Because of her experience as a teacher and learning coach, she has learned how to do the work successfully. Maren is passionate about helping other educators implement, coach, and lead through the PLC process.

In 2020, Maren received the Rebecca Burnette DuFour Scholarship, which celebrates ten women educators across the United States who demonstrate exceptional leadership in their school communities. Using her experience as an educator and Solution Tree associate, she has successfully presented to the Utah State Board of Education as well as many districts, schools, and conferences across the United States, focusing on the implementation of the PLC process as a teacher and coach.

Maren earned a bachelor's degree in English education from Utah Tech University and a master's degree in educational leadership with an endorsement in school leadership from Southern Utah University.

Sheline Miller is a high school assistant principal. She is the former learning coach for the Washington County School District in Utah. She successfully worked with teachers and teams to help establish the practices that led to two schools' recognition as Model PLC schools: (1) Fossil Ridge Intermediate School and (2) Washington Fields Intermediate School in Washington, Utah.

Sheline has served as lead learning coach in her large district to help bring clarity and consistency to teams from school to school. She is also the lead instructor for a leadership certification titled *Leading in a PLC*.

Sheline frequently hosts learning walks of her school for visiting schools and districts, showcasing the work of a true PLC. She was honored to address the Utah State Board of Education, sharing the impact PLCs have on student learning and success, as well as present to the Washington County School Board, showcasing increased teacher efficacy and its relation to embedded best practices focused on the four critical questions of a PLC.

Sheline earned a bachelor's degree from Brigham Young University and a master's degree with an emphasis in school leadership from Southern Utah University.

To book Bob Sonju, Maren Powers, or Sheline Miller for professional development, contact pd@SolutionTree.com.

Foreword:
The Unexpected Depth of Simplicity

BY MIKE MATTOS

I first learned about the Professional Learning Community at Work® process in 2002 at a staff-development day presented by Dr. Richard DuFour at the Orange County Department of Education. Honestly, I did not enter the conference room that October morning of my own free will or with hope that I would learn something useful. My previous years in the profession had taught me that educational reform initiatives come and go about as often as middle school fashion trends, and I assumed that PLCs would be no different. As a first-year elementary school principal, I was surprised that our new superintendent was requiring principals to attend this training since our site plans were due to the school board by the end of the week. So with low expectations and an urgent deadline looming, I strategically placed myself in the back row of the room—out of my superintendent's direct line of sight—and planned to work stealthily on my school site plan. Seven hours later my professional life was indelibly changed for the better.

What resonated with me about the PLC at Work process, and why I believe that the PLC movement has grown exponentially over the past twenty-five years, is the common-sense simplicity of the practices. Three big ideas guide a PLC (DuFour, DuFour, Eaker, Many, & Mattos, 2016).

1. **A focus on learning:** Our school was not built so educators have a place to teach. We are here to ensure our students actually learn the essential academic knowledge, skills, and behaviors needed for their future success. This means our professional practices, policies and procedures should be guided by what is proven to best increase student achievement.

2. **A collaborative culture:** If our mission is to ensure every student learns at high levels, there is no way an individual teacher has all the skills, knowledge, and time required to meet the diverse needs of all their assigned students. Our staff must work collaboratively and take collective responsibility for each student's success.

3. **A results orientation:** Hoping our students learn is not enough; we must know if every student is mastering the essential academic and behavior outcomes needed for future success. This timely information will help guide our actions to support each student.

Who would not want to work at a school where the adults are committed to student success, work together to achieve this noble goal, and collect timely information to guide and affirm their efforts? To me, that would be professional nirvana.

When educators commit to working collaboratively to ensure student learning, four critical questions drive their professional collaboration (DuFour et al., 2016, p. 36).

1. **"What knowledge, skills, and dispositions should every student acquire as a result of this unit, this course, or this grade level?"** We must have clarity and agreement on exactly what all students must learn in each grade or course to be ready for the following year. If we do not have that, how can we work together to ensure all students learn?

2. **"How will we know when each student has acquired the essential knowledge and skills?"** We must know which students have learned each essential standard and which have not learned it yet. If we don't know, how can we identify students who need extra help?

3. **"How will we respond when some students do not learn?"** Some students are going to need additional time and support to learn the essential curriculum. If we don't provide effective extra help, how will we achieve our mission of all students learning at high levels?

4. **"How will we extend the learning for students who are already proficient?"** Because we are committed to all students learning at the highest level possible, shouldn't we extend the learning even further for those who have mastered the essential curriculum?

These four questions are not complicated, confusing, or controversial. This elegant simplicity makes the PLC process both logical and compelling.

Upon my return to campus—and after finishing the site plan—I shared what I had learned with the staff. Not surprisingly, the process resonated with most of the faculty and we embarked on the journey to becoming a professional learning community. As we started to collectively answer the four critical questions, an unexpected obstacle became very clear: doing the work of a PLC was not nearly as straightforward as the process appeared. Ideas can be simple enough to understand, but that does not mean they are easy to do. Just below the surface of simplicity was a challenging depth of complexity.

Like pulling on a sweater's loose thread, our initial attempts to answer each critical question led to other questions that we had to consider. For example, we assumed that answering the first critical question would be very straightforward: *What knowledge, skills, and dispositions should every student acquire as a result of this unit, this course, or this grade level?* We started by asking each grade-level team to review their state English language arts curriculum and create a list of the most essential reading standards that all students must learn to be prepared for the following year. When we pulled on the thread of critical question one, this is what we discovered.

- Team members had markedly different opinions regarding what standards were essential. This disagreement led to our faculty studying the research regarding the characteristics of an essential standard.

- Team members agreed that a specific standard was essential, but had different interpretations regarding the standard's exact meaning. This required the team to collectively define the standard's key terms and determine the specific skills and knowledge that students had to learn.

- Team members agreed on the meaning of an essential standard, but had different opinions regarding the rigor that students had to demonstrate in order to be grade-level proficient. This forced our teams to review the standard vertically—previous year and next year—to determine how students would meet their grade-level expectations.

- Team members agreed on a standard's level of rigor, but could not agree on how to commonly assess students. This need was addressed by improving our collective knowledge on assessment design and determining what format best measured specific levels of rigor.

- Teams agreed on how to commonly assess students, but had not agreed to common pacing for the unit. It would be impossible to share students for interventions unless essential standards were taught at about the same time.

What we thought was a very simple question—*What knowledge, skills, and dispositions should every student acquire as a result of this unit, this course, or this grade level?*—actually had unexpected layers of nuance. Failure to address these facets of the question would cripple our ability to ensure all students learn. And candidly, some teams struggled with this unanticipated complexity and became frustrated and wavered in their commitment to the process. Successfully navigating these rough waters, and extending the simplicity of the PLC at Work process to the actual work of teacher teams, is the purpose of this outstanding book.

The authors of this resource—Bob Sonju, Maren Powers, and Sheline Miller—are exceptional educators who have collectively led multiple schools to record levels of student achievement and Model PLC status. Like my experience, their faculties initially struggled with the unexpected complexities of the work. But their schools embraced that being a true professional learning community is a never-ending process of adult learning and continuous improvement. Through focused collaboration and persistence, they developed processes and tools to simplify the complex work of teacher teams. Their priceless learning created this powerful resource to support team collaboration, accelerate adult learning, and increase your students' achievement.

As you begin to utilize this outstanding book, let me offer a final piece of advice. The authors have simplified the right work, but it is still just that—*work*. It is not easy to ensure every student learns at high levels. If your goal is to eliminate the need to work hard, then you chose the wrong profession. The key is working hard on the right work, not working hard to figure out what you need to do in the first place. This book is your road map to working more efficiently and successfully on the things that will make you a better teacher and your students better learners. Good luck!

Introduction

Simplicity.

As educators, we are acutely aware of the rarity of that in education, especially amid the increasing educational noise that permeates classrooms and schools each day. Educators often find themselves navigating a complex web of demands, expectations, and responsibilities that can hinder the reason they chose teaching as a profession. We are also aware of the dramatic impact that embedding the *professional learning community* (PLC) process has on teacher satisfaction and student learning. We seek to help fellow educators bridge the knowing-doing gap by making the work of a PLC understandable and doable and, in essence, *simplifying* the work. *Simplifying the Journey* is not just another handbook; it's a road map for significant shifts in teacher and team professional practices that contribute to increases in student learning.

Here, you will find an abundance of strategies and tools to make the work of your team and school more efficient and effective. Each chapter will detail an essential, practical action that you will be able to immediately implement into your daily practice.

Too often, during the school year, educators are met with a lack of clarity regarding their school's and team's work. As a result, everyone can feel swallowed up by new initiatives and slowly retreat to the privacy of their classroom, close the door, and teach. This lack of clarity and the resulting retreat are a problem. We can change the prevalence of ambiguity and replace it with simple actions that leaders, teachers, and teams can take to increase their collective learning and that of their students.

However, we cannot improve student learning without the adults in the building changing their behaviors. While holding that truth in mind, the authors of this book (passionate practitioners who understand the overwhelming demands placed on educators and leaders and have endured years of endless change initiatives) have this as their response to the passionate plea of educators everywhere to "please make this simple and doable!"

This book shares a process that simplifies the work of teams and leaders with resources and examples to move forward your team's, school's, or district's work around the four critical questions of a PLC at Work®:

> 1. **What knowledge, skills, and dispositions should every student acquire as a result of this unit, this course, or this grade level?**
>
> 2. **How will we know when each student has acquired the essential knowledge and skills?**
>
> 3. **How will we respond when some students do not learn?**
>
> 4. **How will we extend the learning for students who are already proficient? (DuFour, DuFour, Eaker, Many, & Mattos, 2016, p. 36)**

Instead of treating these four critical questions as separate pieces, this book treats them as integral parts of a process and works to streamline "the interconnectedness of these characteristics" (Eaker, 2020, p. 139).

Simplifying the Journey supports the work of two distinct K–12 educators—(1) the school and team leader (for collaborative teams) and (2) the instructional coach—since each of these professionals is essential to significantly changing a school's practices, yet each requires a slightly different approach. Further, this book challenges your thinking regarding your school's and teams' work, teaches you a process that is proven to make a difference in both student and teacher learning, and articulates what the work looks like as schools and teams connect.

Simplifying the Journey is divided into chapters, each dedicated to describing a step in the process with specific actions teams and schools can take to answer each of the four critical questions to ensure high levels of learning for all students and educators and truly engage in the PLC process. The seventh chapter is what is required for the six actions to work.

- **Chapter 1:** Identifying essential standards and skills (critical question one)

- **Chapter 2:** Gaining shared clarity and clearly defining mastery (critical question one)

- **Chapter 3:** Encouraging student ownership through learning progressions and rubrics (critical question two)

- **Chapter 4:** Utilizing formative assessment for feedback (critical question two)

- **Chapter 5:** Learning from team data (critical questions two, three, and four)

- **Chapter 6:** Creating extra time and support for those who need it (critical questions three and four)

- **Chapter 7:** Ensuring focused, productive collaboration

Each chapter is structured to help teachers, leaders, and instructional coaches understand what the work *is*, how to *lead* the work, and how to *coach* the work. Each chapter is divided into the following sections.

- **The Action** (an introductory anecdote and description of the required action)

- **Leading the Work**—Specific Actions of School and Team Leaders

- **Coaching the Work**—Specific Actions of Learning Coaches

- **Don't Miss This** (things to be aware of while on your journey)

The Action

Simplifying the Journey guides you through six steps that help teams and schools better answer the four critical questions of a PLC. Figure I.1 (page 4) represents each of these steps and their corresponding actions.

Notice there are six essential actions when simplifying the journey. Under each step are targeted questions that serve as reminders for teams and leaders as they engage in the work. It is important to note that each of these actions is not isolated but part of a simplifying process that teams and leaders engage in to clarify the work of answering the four critical questions of a PLC. For example, as teams consider critical question one, "What knowledge, skills, and dispositions should every student acquire as a result of this unit, this course, or this grade level?" (DuFour et al., 2016, p. 36), the work of teams is represented by identifying essential standards and skills (action one) and gaining shared clarity and defining mastery (action two) for each.

Once teams are clear on what all students need to know and have a shared understanding of what mastery will look like, the teams then begin thinking about how to assess where a student is on the path to mastery. This work is represented in the PLC process by critical question two, "How will we know when each student has acquired the essential knowledge and skills?" (DuFour et al., 2016, p. 36). In order for teams to address question two, they must consider multiple assessment practices: creating student ownership through self-assessment (action three), using formative assessment for feedback (action four), and learning from their formative assessment data (action five).

Finally, teams consider how to provide extra time and targeted support (action six) in order for students to either (1) meet mastery of the essential standard or (2) deepen their learning after demonstrating mastery in the essential standard, which addresses critical question three, "How will we respond when some students do not learn?" and critical question four, "How will we extend the learning for students who are already proficient?" (DuFour et al., 2016, p. 36).

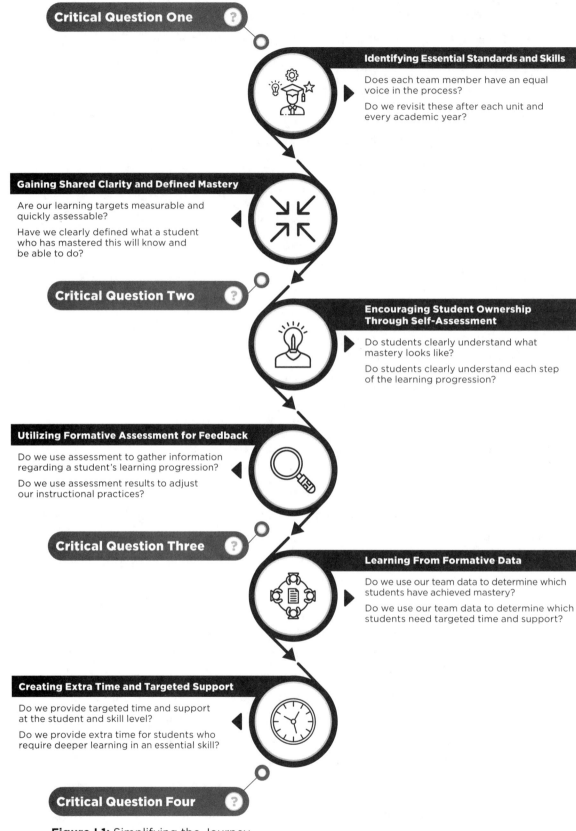

Critical Question One ?

Identifying Essential Standards and Skills

Does each team member have an equal voice in the process?

Do we revisit these after each unit and every academic year?

Gaining Shared Clarity and Defined Mastery

Are our learning targets measurable and quickly assessable?

Have we clearly defined what a student who has mastered this will know and be able to do?

Critical Question Two ?

Encouraging Student Ownership Through Self-Assessment

Do students clearly understand what mastery looks like?

Do students clearly understand each step of the learning progression?

Utilizing Formative Assessment for Feedback

Do we use assessment to gather information regarding a student's learning progression?

Do we use assessment results to adjust our instructional practices?

Critical Question Three ?

Learning From Formative Data

Do we use our team data to determine which students have achieved mastery?

Do we use our team data to determine which students need targeted time and support?

Creating Extra Time and Targeted Support

Do we provide targeted time and support at the student and skill level?

Do we provide extra time for students who require deeper learning in an essential skill?

Critical Question Four ?

Figure I.1: Simplifying the Journey.

These six actions, combined with the tools offered throughout this book, will provide teachers, teams, and leaders with a clear, simplified focus for the day-to-day work of educators.

Along these lines, in parallel with the simplification process, there is our simplified cycle of instruction, or instructional pattern, that teachers and teams can follow as they shift their focus from delivering content throughout the year to ensuring that students learn the identified essential standards and skills outlined in chapter 1 (page 13).

In a traditional cycle of instruction, a teacher will choose what they want to teach, teach it to the students, give an end-of-unit assessment, and record a score in the gradebook. This pattern is often repeated throughout the school year. It's important to note that through this, some students will grasp the concept or skill and others will not, resulting in a certain randomness to student progress. Our simplified cycle of instruction remedies this. Consider the simplified unit of instruction in figure I.2.

Source: Adapted from Buffum, Mattos, & Malone, 2018.

Figure I.2: Unit cycle of instruction.

When teachers and teams plan their unit of instruction, the first step is to identify the essential standards and skills that will be learned during the unit. As teams do this, they articulate the individual learning targets associated with the unit of instruction and agree on what mastery will look like for each.

Next, teams commit to giving team formative assessments throughout the unit of instruction. These assessments provide valuable information to the teacher and team about learning and the impact of their selected teaching strategies. These team formative assessments also provide specific, timely information about which students need extra time and support in target knowledge or skills. This also means teachers and teams don't wait for the end-of-unit assessment to intervene with students. Instead, they find time to support students during the unit, catching misunderstandings and deficiencies throughout.

Finding extra time comes down to rethinking what happens during daily classroom instruction. We recommend adjusting instructional patterns in each unit of instruction to include a day (or days, depending on the unit's length) when no new instruction occurs. We recommend that the teacher and team commit to a day (or more, depending on the unit's length) for students to receive extra time and support. Again, on this day, no new instruction is provided. Instead, the team considers the results of the team formative assessment, identifies those strategies that proved to be most effective, divides students among the team based on need (intervention or extended learning), and utilizes the instructional time to provide targeted help or extend learning opportunities. Following this, instruction and formative assessment continue in preparation for the end-of-unit assessment. This simple instructional cycle provides a framework for teams as they plan for their units of instruction.

Leading the Work—
Specific Actions of School and Team Leaders

School and team leaders need to relentlessly reduce the educational noise surrounding our teachers, be leery of adding more to educators' already overflowing plates, and passionately focus on providing clarity, effective monitoring, and support for the work proven to increase student learning and teacher efficacy. In their study of transformational schools, authors Jayson W. Richardson, Justin Bathon, and Scott McLeod (2021) borrow from researchers to characterize what types of leaders are critical to transforming a school: "At the root of every one of these transforming schools are courageous individuals who are leading the change. They are discontent with the status quo and are willing to rethink fundamental concepts of schooling" (p. 4).

Note that the authors of the study use the word *individuals* as they describe those needed for change (Richardson et al., 2021). Change most certainly does not solely depend on a principal or a courageous educator who single-handedly alters a school's culture and practices. Instead, it takes those who are dissatisfied with the status quo, those who are compelled to challenge the traditional thinking about school. This change requires team and school leaders with the courage to rethink how school is traditionally conducted.

To assist with this change, we strongly encourage that team and school leaders follow a pattern of four leadership actions to move the work of teachers, teams, and the school forward. The Leading the Work section in each chapter provides specific, proven strategies for leading this work and supporting teams' work through the four essential leadership actions (DuFour, n.d.).

1. **Clarify and communicate the work:** It's essential for school and team leaders to clearly articulate what the work looks like and consistently communicate this to teachers and teams. Often, this clarification and communication centers on why the work should be done. Research and logic-based reasoning give leaders the communication points they can use to communicate why.

2. **Support teachers as they learn together:** Changing the way things are done requires varied types of support as teachers and teams change habits and learn new practices. As such, teachers need the necessary time, resources, and coaching.

3. **Monitor the work:** As teams and leaders build a culture of learning together, it's important to clarify that this action is not a call to micromanage teams. Instead, *monitor the work* means team and school leaders model the practice of learning together by consistently asking guiding questions in order to do two things: (1) identify and celebrate the strengths of the team and (2) pinpoint target areas where the team could benefit from coaching assistance.

4. **Validate and celebrate teams as they learn:** Frequent recognition and validation are essential feedback to teachers and teams, serving as necessary motivation as they implement and accomplish the work.

For school and team leaders, these four foundational leadership keys will provide a predictable pattern to follow as they ensure clarity, support, and validation as teachers and teams engage in this work. These keys are described in greater detail in each chapter.

Coaching the Work— Specific Actions of Learning Coaches

Throughout *Simplifying the Journey*, teachers and teams are guided through the work of collective inquiry and learning. In his book *The Impact Cycle: What Instructional Coaches Should Do to Foster Powerful Improvements in Teaching*, Jim Knight (2018) sets up a cyclical pattern for coaching: (1) identify, (2) learn, and (3) improve. This cyclical pattern of inquiry, practice, and reflection is mirrored in the coaching section of each chapter of *Simplifying the Journey*.

Coaches keep teams on their intended path, helping them adjust and course-correct. This often requires changing practices, perceptions of student learning and ability, and the ways teachers interact. A transformational coach goes deeper than mere behaviors, delving into beliefs and systems change (Aguilar, 2013).

As team members work together to answer the four critical questions, keep in mind the three big ideas of a PLC: (1) a focus on learning, (2) a collaborative culture and collective responsibility, and (3) a results orientation (DuFour et al., 2016). This book provides a framework in which to use that focus. The following appears in each Coaching the Work section.

- **Consider this scenario:** A scenario in each chapter describes the beliefs and practices of a fictional team. Although fictitious, each scenario presents an opportunity to reflect on ways to move the team forward in their work. It is important that coaches identify each team's strengths and challenges, as well as next steps.

- **Plan and gather evidence:** Coaches will assist teams as they outline a plan of action and as they gather data to mark progress. A clear plan aligned with steps in the simplified process ensures that teachers, teams, and ultimately the school are working toward the same end. Specific instructions help coaches clearly guide teams through this process. Various examples and resources provide help during the process. Question banks in these sections provide thought provokers and action planners. Use these questions to gain insight into elements that are currently in place and to identify and develop next steps. Don't be limited by the questions posed in each chapter. Instead, use them as a launching pad to foster deep and thoughtful discussion.

- **Reflect to elicit change:** Reviewing the results of the actions (whether successful or not) helps teams learn and helps coaches decide what support teams and teachers need from different sources (be it from the coach, other teachers, or administrators) to strategically move forward. Team action inventories appear in this section and, chapter by chapter, build the reproducible "Team Coaching Inventory" (page 10). As you coach, you ask teams to commit to one action to start doing, one action to stop doing, and one action to continue doing. Establishing a team SMART goal at the conclusion of each chapter directs the work also.

SMART goals include the following characteristics (Conzemius & O'Neill, 2014).

Strategic and specific: Your goal is clearly defined and states exactly what you are going to achieve.

Measurable: Your goal states success criteria so you can track progress and know when your goal is met.

Attainable: Your goal challenges you but is also something realistic.

Results oriented: Your goal is connected to what is valuable and important to your team.

Time bound: Your goal includes a date you will have achieved it by.

We are confident that at this book's conclusion, you will have a solid coaching plan of action to follow for the year that will help teams maintain focus on the processes outlined in *Simplifying the Journey.*

Don't Miss This

There's a proverb that is often remembered this way: "To know the road ahead, ask those coming back."

At the conclusion of each chapter, we share a few words of wisdom to be mindful of at each step of your journey. Consider these reminders, cautions, and encouragements from those who have traveled the road.

There is nothing in this book's title or pages that indicates this work will be easy. *Simplifying the Journey* is not about quick fixes or flashy shortcuts. It is about leveraging effective practices and strategies that are proven to increase the learning of students and educators. We acknowledge that changing behaviors and practices is tough work. *Simplifying the Journey* was written *by* educators and leaders *for* educators and leaders. In it are shared simplified actions to spur a different mindset. Improving a school is not about working harder—educators are some of the hardest-working people on the planet. Instead, *Simplifying the Journey* is a process to help educators simplify their workload and amplify their collective impact on students. Join us as we reimagine your collective practices in the classroom, within your team, and in your school. Now, let's learn together!

Team Coaching Inventory

Directions: After reading each chapter, assess your team's current reality for each step by recording an action you will start, an action you will stop, and an action you will continue. Finish by writing a SMART goal and a reflection for each step.

ACTION ONE: ESSENTIAL STANDARDS AND SKILLS

START	STOP	CONTINUE

SMART Goal

Reflection

ACTION TWO: SHARED CLARITY AND DEFINED MASTERY

START	STOP	CONTINUE

SMART Goal

Reflection

ACTION THREE: STUDENT OWNERSHIP AND LEARNING PROGRESSIONS

START	STOP	CONTINUE

SMART Goal

Reflection

ACTION FOUR: FORMATIVE ASSESSMENT FOR FEEDBACK	START	STOP	CONTINUE

SMART Goal	

Reflection	

ACTION FIVE: LEARNING FROM FORMATIVE DATA	START	STOP	CONTINUE

SMART Goal	

Reflection	

ACTION SIX: EXTRA TIME AND SUPPORT	START	STOP	CONTINUE

SMART Goal	

Reflection	

FOCUSED COLLABORATION	START	STOP	CONTINUE

SMART Goal	

Reflection	

Answering critical question one:

"What knowledge, skills, and dispositions should

every student acquire as a result of this unit,

this course, or this grade level?"

(DuFour et al., 2016, p. 36)

1

Identifying Essential Standards and Skills

Teachers understand that in most content areas, the sheer number of standards presents several major professional problems. Delivering these standards in the time provided during a traditional school year is nearly impossible. Compounding this challenge is the fact that most content standards are complex, with a variety of parts requiring a student to demonstrate multiple skills to master each standard.

Most content areas have some standards woven into the overall set of standards that teachers consider nice to know, while they would deem other standards absolutely essential for the students to know and be able to do. Those are *essential standards*. They are important for a student to know in order to succeed in the course, the grade level, and beyond.

We strongly believe that the professional experts who deliver the standards in the classroom—the teacher teams—should be the ones who identify essential standards and skills. After teams identify and come to consensus on the essential standards, it's critical that they revisit each of these at the end of each unit and also each academic year. Be cautious of viewing this as a task you complete. Resist the urge to laminate the identified essential standards and never revisit them. Instead, see this work as an opportunity to learn and grow as a team. Each unit of instruction provides new perspectives regarding essential standards, and although what is essential may not change dramatically, the collective unique perspectives provide opportunities to discuss what the essential standards expect of students, what mastery looks like, and what assessment methods are possible.

Keep in mind that the essential standards are not the only standards that teachers will give instruction on during a school year. They are the standards on which they focus collaborative formative assessments and targeted extra time and support.

Leading the Work— Specific Actions of School and Team Leaders

Leaders can take the following specific actions to clarify and communicate the work to be accomplished; support teachers as they learn together; monitor the work; and validate and celebrate teams as they learn to identify essential standards and skills.

Clarify and Communicate the Work

One of the biggest mistakes a leader can make is to simply announce, "Teachers, you need to identify standards that are essential and turn them in to me by next week!" This proclamation, however well-intentioned, is fraught with problems and absolutely doomed to fail. Instead, begin by making a compelling case for why the need exists to determine essential standards and skills (as outlined at the beginning of this chapter). Their identification is critical to forming effective teams and foundational to ensuring all students learn because a team's focus turns from attempting to *teach* all the standards to ensuring all students *learn* a specific set of standards and skills critical for success in the course or grade level. This shift in collective practice is a critical first action of teams. Instead of having individual teachers develop pacing guides focused on teaching all the standards in a course or grade level, teams collectively engage in studying the standards, prioritizing those that are essential.

We do not advocate for eliminating standards. Instead, this action expects that teachers will adjust their practices by doing the following.

- Studying the standards together using the professional perspectives, experiences, and wisdom of all members of the team

- Prioritizing standards by identifying a certain set that are essential for success in the course or grade level

- Forgoing the ineffective practice of trying to cover all the standards and replacing it with working to ensure all students master those deemed essential

Instead of announcing a mandate to teachers and teams, leaders must engage in constructive conversations with teachers and teams by posing guiding questions like the following, which seek to find common ground and shared agreement.

- "What is the biggest challenge you face with the number of standards you are called on to teach each year?"

- "If you believe there is enough time during the school year to deliver the standards in your content area and to have every student learn them, can you break down that timeline?"

- "As individual teachers, how are you intentionally or unintentionally giving priority to some standards?"

- "What value is there in a team agreeing on which standards are essential?"

- "What benefits would you see in shifting from delivering curriculum to agreeing on and focusing instruction on standards that you collectively deem essential?"

Advise teachers to consider their content colleagues. There is likely to be agreement in some areas and wildly different expectations in others. That is because teachers bring various experiences, perspectives, backgrounds, and expertise to the conversation. In the end, the perspectives and expertise can blend, and teachers can come to a shared agreement.

Support Teachers as They Learn Together

A common refrain teachers voice is, "We need more time." In order to engage in the work of identifying essential standards, teachers need time and supportive coaching to learn together. It's disingenuous for leaders to call on teachers to engage in the critical work of identifying essential standards without also providing the time and support (and caffeinated beverages) needed to do this ongoing work for every unit of instruction and throughout the year.

Ideas for creating time for teams to engage in this work follow.

- Building common prep periods into the school's master schedule

- Using flexible funds to compensate teachers for completing the work

- Providing substitute teachers for classes releasing teachers and teams to do this work

- Covering a team's assembly responsibilities with support staff and releasing teams to do this work

- Coordinating early-out or late-start days

Creating time for teachers and teams to engage in this work requires some ingenuity. Your school or district's response to providing time for teachers is limited only by your creativity.

Teams and leaders can utilize the following question framework to deem which standards are essential (Many & Horrell, 2022).

- **Readiness:** Will the standard provide students with the knowledge they need to be ready for the next course or grade level?

- **Endurance:** Will knowledge of the standard provide students with knowledge or skills needed beyond the unit of study?

- **Assessed:** Is knowledge of the standard highly likely to be reflected in a large portion of a high-stakes assessment the students will take?

- **Leverage:** Will knowledge of the standard potentially have value in other courses or disciplines?

Prioritizing standards also helps to ensure consistency from classroom to classroom while providing teams with a focus for assessment and collaborative efforts. It's important to note that the essential standards are not the only things that educators teach during the year. They are, however, the standards and skills that teams formatively assess and provide extra time and support to ensure that all students learn. They serve as the foundation for a team's collaborative work.

Monitor the Work

As you begin this part of the process, keep in mind that the way you interact with your team as a leader is vital to its success. Being thoughtful with your actions and comments, humble enough to listen to and learn from others, and knowledgeable about the process will help you succeed with your team.

Evidence of prioritized standards with a list of those deemed essential is the key to monitoring the identification and implementation of essential standards. Again, asking the following targeted questions and communicating what evidence you expect helps you monitor where a team is in the process of identifying and implementing essential standards in the classroom.

- "Is there agreement regarding which standards are essential for all students to know and be able to do?"

- "Has each teacher had an equal voice in the process?"

- "Are teachers who are new to the team given the opportunity to provide a different perspective on the essential standards?"

- "What evidence does your team have that the essential standards have been learned?"

- "Is your team revisiting the essential standards at the end of each unit and throughout the year?"

These targeted questions are meant to create a productive dialogue for the leader and team while providing valuable insight into the successes each team is experiencing and the challenges they are facing. This ongoing information allows the leader to provide the targeted support needed for the team to overcome setbacks.

Validate and Celebrate Teams as They Learn

More than cheesecake and caffeine (although both are nice), recognition and validation of this work are critical for leaders to provide and for teams to receive. Keep in mind that teachers and teams are growing professionally in this process and will require constant encouragement, feedback, and validation as they learn together. Often it takes a simple action from the leader to validate and inspire the teachers and teams to continue this important work.

Here are a few ways to celebrate and validate this work.

- **Power of the sticky note:** Very few things are as influential as validation of our professional work. Writing a note recognizing the work a teacher has engaged in and putting the note on the teacher's desk is an act of validation.

- **Learning together:** As team and school leaders encourage the practice of learning together, it is often validating to recognize a team for their work by asking them to briefly share their work and what they learned.

- **In-house professional learning:** Some of the best professional learning takes place when teachers and teams share their practices with their colleagues. Often, team members struggle with the same kinds of challenges. Providing opportunities for teams that have successfully engaged in this work to help their peers encourages a sense of unity and a culture of learning together.

- **Dine and shine:** Who doesn't love a free lunch? Working with a parent-teacher organization, a school community council, or community businesses to provide lunch for a team and celebrate team successes can serve to validate and celebrate the work of the team.

Coaching the Work—
Specific Actions of Learning Coaches

Coaching teachers through this work requires supporting them in their efforts to prioritize the essential skills and guiding them through any misconceptions. This is what will begin to create real change in schools.

Consider This Scenario

A team of history teachers is meeting to discuss what they will be teaching during the upcoming year. They have been tasked with giving curricular priority to the essential standards and skills in their curriculum. Teacher A has brought a copy of the core state standards and is ready to discuss which skills should be taught. He also has the lessons he taught the previous year to use to select important skills. Teacher B has also brought a copy of the core standards and has done the work of ranking the skills within each strand from

continued →

most important to least important. She, too, has her previous lessons but already knows some of the lessons she loves don't fit well with her rankings. Teacher C didn't feel the need to bring a copy of the core standards because he views all the standards as essential; otherwise, they wouldn't be included. As such, Teacher C views this work as a waste of time because he feels compelled to cover everything in the standards.

The team does have the following strengths.

- Teachers A and B are aware of the core standards.

- Teacher A is prepared with previous lessons and seems willing to discuss what is required to move forward.

- Teacher B seems ready to streamline the curriculum standards and realizes she may need to rework or reprioritize some of her favorite lessons.

To identify some of the obstacles this team is facing, consider the following challenge areas.

- Teacher C appears resistant to engaging in the discussion of giving priority to certain standards and skills because, from his perspective, they are all important. After prioritizing, teams shift their focus from covering all the standards in a hurry to teaching, assessing, and intervening on a certain set of standards. Determining essential standards and skills will focus the teaching practices and free up time to help students.

- Teacher A seems amenable to deconstructing the core, but ultimately just wants to use the same things that have been used in the classroom year after year because they're comfortable.

Coaching considerations for this team follow.

- **Don't toss out everything:** Encourage teams to use lessons they have but adjust them to better align with the identified essential standards.

- **Learn from mistakes instead of ignoring them:** Be cautious about encouraging teams to simply eliminate their past lessons. Instead, encourage teams to rethink, redesign, or modify existing lessons to better align with the essential standards.

Plan and Gather Evidence

Have teams commit to at least one full day in this action of the process between April and June to help prepare for the coming year. While a content-specific team can likely achieve this in a single day, elementary teachers need more time because they have multiple content areas. Have elementary teachers focus on one subject per year until they have evaluated all subjects. This prevents them from being overwhelmed. This step and the subsequent steps should occur on a frequent basis.

Also, it is imperative that each teacher on the team participate in the process, creating the commitment and collective promise needed as a team. While it may seem daunting at first and (full disclosure) it does end in what feels like a long day, the time investment made during this work will pay dividends in preparation and confidence when the school year begins. Your team will gain a shared understanding of the standards and take the first step toward gaining the sense that you are all rowing at the same time in the same direction.

To coach the team as they perform this step for the first time and in subsequent cycles, take the following steps.

1. **Have the team select a day when their only goal is to determine essential standards and skills.** Ask them to commit to revisiting this each academic year and reflecting on the successes and weaknesses of each unit after each assessment. To prepare, teams need the following items.

    → A meeting agenda to keep everyone on the same page (See the reproducible "Identifying the Essential Standards—Meeting Agenda," page 29, for a template.)

    → Your content area's testing blueprint, if available

    → Your standards, each written in a large font size so there is one standard per sheet of paper

    → One copy of the reproducible "Identifying the Essential Standards and Skills Cards" (page 32) for each teacher and each standard (The team members can instead do this work in a shared document if the team is tight on paper.)

    → The reproducible "Team Essential Standards Guide" (page 33) to capture the team's agreed-on essentials and to serve as a critical resource for the team throughout the year

2. **Create norms for the work.** Make sure the team is present and ready to work together toward standards and skills that are essential for your students next year. This means making sure you have team norms set up for that year. Why? This allows for every member of the team to act as a vital member. It also makes sure that every person is participating equally. See page 148 for more information about norm creation.

3. **When they are ready, have the essential standards either spread out on desks or taped to a board so that the team can easily view and evaluate them.** For examples of what this looks like in actual meetings, see figure 1.1 (page 20) and figure 1.2 (page 21).

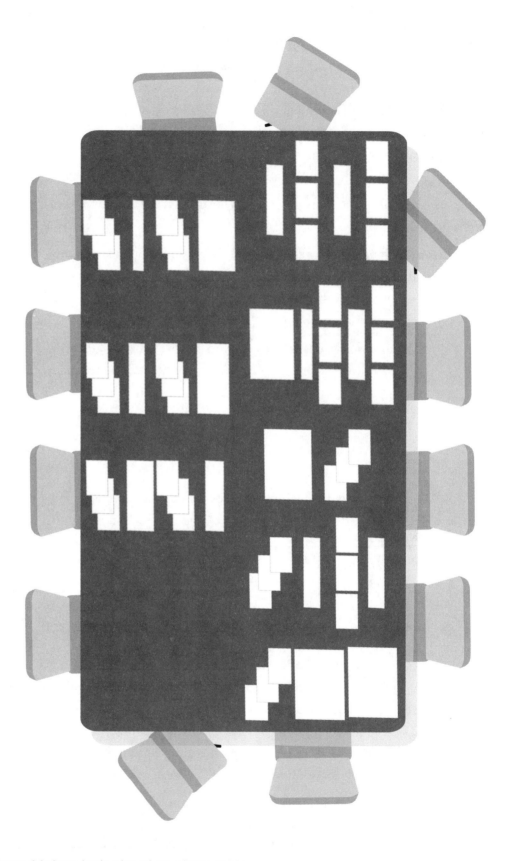

Figure 1.1: Standards placed on a large table.

Standard 7-8.W:

Students will learn to write for a variety of tasks, purposes, and audiences using appropriate grammar/conventions, syntax, and style.

Standard 7-8.W.1:

Write arguments to support claims with clear reasons and relevant evidence, and provide a conclusion that follows from and supports the argument presented.

a. Introduce claim(s), acknowledge and distinguish the claim(s) from alternate or opposing claims, and organize the reasons and evidence logically.

b. Support claim(s) with logical reasoning and relevant evidence, using accurate, credible sources.

c. Use precise words, phrases, clauses, and modifiers to create cohesion and clarify the relationships among claim(s), counterclaims, reasons, and evidence.

d. Establish and maintain a style appropriate to the audience, purpose, and task, including the use of verbs in the active and passive voice and in the conditional and subjunctive mood.

e. Use commas, ellipses, or dashes as appropriate within writing.

Standard 7-8.W.2:

Write informative/explanatory texts to examine a topic and convey ideas, concepts, and information through the selection, organization, and analysis of relevant content, and provide a conclusion that supports the information or explanation presented.

a. Introduce a topic clearly, previewing what is to follow; organize ideas, concepts, and information into broader categories; include formatting, graphics, and multimedia when useful.

b. Develop the topic with relevant facts, definitions, concrete details, quotations, and examples.

c. Use appropriate and varied transitions to create cohesion and clarify the relationships among ideas and concepts.

d. Use precise language and content-specific vocabulary to inform about or explain the topic.

e. Establish and maintain a style appropriate to the audience, purpose, and task, including the use of verbs in the active and passive voice and in the conditional and subjunctive mood.

f. Use commas, ellipses, or dashes as appropriate within writing.

Source for standard: Utah State Office of Education, 2013.

Figure 1.2: Standards taped to a whiteboard.

4. **Have each teacher on the team go through and complete the reproducible "Identifying the Essential Standards and Skills Cards" (page 32) for each standard on their own.** Again, they can do this with actual note cards or a shared document. While the cards are helpful visuals and can keep the teachers anonymous, the shared document works when paper and time are in short supply. For real-life examples using the same standard written by three different teachers, see figure 1.3, and for different standards on the same piece of paper, see figure 1.4.

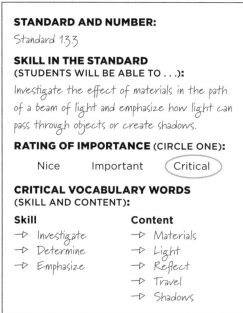
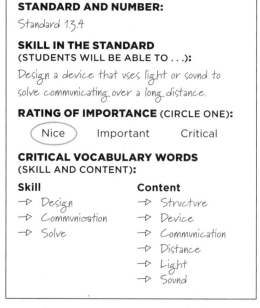

Figure 1.3: "Identifying the Essential Standards and Skills Cards"—Elementary science example on a single document.

SKILL IN THE STANDARD (STUDENTS WILL BE ABLE TO . . .)**:**

Write arguments to support claims with relevant evidence.

RATING OF IMPORTANCE (CIRCLE ONE)**:**

Not at All				Very
1	2	3	4	(5)

Vocabulary

→ Evidence   → Credible sources

→ Claims   → Logical reasoning

SKILL IN THE STANDARD (STUDENTS WILL BE ABLE TO . . .)**:**

Write for a variety of tasks, purposes, and audiences. No minimum length is stated, just tasks.

RATING OF IMPORTANCE (CIRCLE ONE)**:**

Not at All				Very
1	2	3	4	(5)

Vocabulary

→ Opposing claims   → Grammar focus

→ Credible sources   → Ellipses, comma

→ Counterclaim   → Dash

→ Logical evidence

SKILL IN THE STANDARD (STUDENTS WILL BE ABLE TO . . .)**:**

Write an argumentative essay with relevant evidence, credible sources, correct grammar, and an opposing claim.

RATING OF IMPORTANCE (CIRCLE ONE)**:**

Not at All				Very
1	2	3	4	(5)

Vocabulary

→ Counterclaim   → Credible

→ Evidence   → Relevant

→ Purpose

Source: © 2023 by Kathryn Guisinger and Aymee DeLaPaz. Used with permission.

Figure 1.4: A variation of "Identifying the Essential Standards and Skills Cards"—Secondary English language arts example on individual cards.

5. **Someone in the meeting reads each reviewed standard and the feedback on each card, and the members come to a consensus on the priority.** If they decide it is important or critical to know, it is an essential standard and skill set, and the team commits to assessing it and intervening on it.

6. **After determining essential standards and skills, the team completes the "Team Essential Standards Guide" (page 33), an example of which is in figure 1.5.** This provides a blueprint for the year, laying out learning targets, when they will be assessed, what the essential vocabulary is, what feedback prompts teachers will use, and what mastery looks like for each skill. (The shaded area of figure 2.13 is completed in the next chapter, on page 52.) Make a specific plan to move the members in the same direction. Initially, this could include an analysis of current material driven by questions like these.

   → Which lesson plans align with the essential skills and need no modifications?

   → Which lesson plans have elements of the essential skills but need modifications to properly teach an essential skill?

   → Which lesson plans can supplement learning for those who have already mastered the essential skills?

7. **The team writes, in their own words, those standards that they agree are essential and reference the agreed-on vocabulary.** Next to the learning targets (which are addressed in chapter 2, page 35), they put the number of the associated standard. They may combine or omit some learning targets based on what is critical, important, or nice to know.

8. **Encourage the team to share these essential standards with the grade level above and the grade level below theirs.** This is a catalyst for productive vertical conversations from grade to grade, with a focus on what students need to know on each step of their learning journey.

Team: First grade (science)		Year: 2024		
INSTRUCTIONAL PACING	**ESSENTIAL STANDARD**	**ACADEMIC VOCABULARY**	**FORMATIVE FEEDBACK PROMPTS**	**LEARNING TARGETS AND MASTERY**
Provide the month in which you will teach the essential standards and skills. *(Pacing guide)*	List the agreed-on essential standards and skills for the course or grade level. *(Those critical for all students)*	List the critical academic vocabulary that students will need to know. *(Vocabulary front-loaded prior to instruction)*	List formative feedback questions used to assess and provide feedback during instruction. *(Information-gathering prompts)*	List learning targets and describe what a proficient student will know and be able to do. *(Targets for all students)*
August (First Week)	**ESS 3A:** I can investigate to show the cause-and-effect relationship between sound and vibrating matter.			
August (Second Week)	**ESS 3B:** I can use a model to show the effect of light on objects to either illuminate them or give their own light off.			
August (Third Week)	**ESS 3C:** I can investigate the effect of materials in the path of a beam of light and emphasize how light can pass through objects or create shadows.			
August–September (Fourth Week / First Week)	**ESS 3D:** I can design a device that uses light or sound to solve communicating over a long distance.			

Source for standard: Nebraska State Board of Education, 2017.

Figure 1.5: Team essential standards guide, elementary example.

The question bank in figure 1.6 includes a series of guiding questions to help teams inventory what they do and do not have in their current practices regarding essential standards and skills. Use these guiding questions as a launching pad to drill down to the truly essential.

What vertical alignment with the grades above and below do you have access to, and can you use them to help determine which skills to deem as essential?	Can you articulate the learning targets?
	Do the learning targets align with the core?
Has the team determined whether the skills are critical, important, or nice to know?	Do the learning targets align with the end-of-level tests?
	What skills will students be able to use going forward?
What do you really want from your students in the areas of learning, behavior, and engagement?	Have students learned skills in a previous grade?
	What is critical vocabulary from the core?
What will students look like, sound like, and be doing as they work toward mastery?	What skills are unique or introduced this year?
	Will students learn skills again in another grade or class?

Figure 1.6: Question bank—Essential standards and skills.

Reflect to Elicit Change

Honest introspection and reflection will lead to next steps. Based on teams' current reality and data, a coach can help teams reflect on their learning with the following questions and complete the first part of the team coaching inventory in figure 1.7.

- **Start doing:** What practice or type of thinking can the team immediately start doing to move forward in this process?

- **Stop doing:** What practice or type of thinking can the team stop doing because it does not align with the intended outcomes of their decisions?

- **Continue doing:** What practice or type of thinking can the team celebrate and keep doing?

		START	STOP	CONTINUE
ACTION ONE: ESSENTIAL STANDARDS AND SKILLS		Identifying the essential standards or skills needed to be successful in the course or grade level	Testing the entire core! (Focus on the skills that are essential for the current grade level.)	Using our collective strengths by tweaking and sharing effective strategies that have been successful in the past
SMART Goal		As a team, inventory our previous lessons (unit by unit) to find the ones that can be used and the ones that need to be deleted from our Tier 1 instruction one week prior to the start of each unit.		
Reflection		Focusing on the essential skills really helped decrease some of the stress of getting through an entire core before the end of a school year. We aren't quite sure if we hit all of the essentials. We also have a new teacher this next year who will need to be onboarded by completing the process regularly.		

Figure 1.7: Example of team coaching inventory, action one.

Don't Miss This

Be aware of the following things while leading and coaching the journey.

- **Everyone needs a voice:** Significant change comes from honoring the unique perspectives of all members of the team. When identifying essential standards and skills, begin the process by individually considering the priority of each standard. This allows all team thoughts to be captured without the persuasion that may come from a dominant personality. The beauty of learning communities is that wisdom, experience, and multiple perspectives contribute to a rich collective learning experience.

- **This is not a one-and-done process:** Instead, teams should review their essential standards and skills prior to and at the end of every unit of instruction as well as yearly. Each unit that is taught and each unit that is completed adds experience and insight to a team. As such, revisiting essential standards is a cycle that needs to be repeated continually. As teams review, refine, and vertically align the essential standards, the continuity and efficacy of the teams increase, and the question, "What do *all* students need to know and be able to do?" becomes a central focus of their teaching and assessing efforts.

The identification of essential standards and skills is certainly not new thinking in the field of education. Many teams have engaged in this work to varying degrees, which begs the question, "Why hasn't the identification of essential standards improved learning in schools?" Let us be clear: identifying essential standards alone does nothing to increase learning for students or teams' effectiveness. With the complexity and ambiguity of most standards, there will be a myriad of understandings and perspectives regarding what a student who has mastered a standard will know and be able to do. The next action of *Simplifying the Journey* asks teams to gain shared clarity and clearly define mastery regarding each essential standard.

Identifying the Essential Standards—
Meeting Agenda

Date:	Time:

CELEBRATIONS:

NORMS WE COMMIT TO THAT GUIDE OUR WORK:

1.

2.

3.

4.

5.

AS YOU IDENTIFY THE ESSENTIAL STANDARDS, CONSIDER THESE QUESTIONS.

What skills are in each standard?

Which skills are critical to know, important to know, and nice to know?

What is the essential vocabulary for this standard or skill?

What formative feedback prompts go with the specific standard or skill?

Which skills will we assess in addition to all the *critical* skills? Will we assess some or all of the *important* skills? Will we turn *nice-to-know* standards into extensions?

How can we use assessments we already have? Which do we need to modify, and which do we need to create?

Simplifying the Journey © 2024 Solution Tree Press • SolutionTree.com
Visit **go.SolutionTree.com/PLCbooks** to download this free reproducible.

Identifying the Essential Standards and Skills Cards

Standard and Number: _____

Skill in the Standard (students will be able to . . .):

_____

_____

_____

_____

Rating of Importance (circle one):

   Nice   Important   Critical

Critical Vocabulary Words (Skill and Content):

Skill:

- _____
- _____
- _____

Content:

- _____
- _____
- _____

Standard and Number: _____

Skill in the Standard (students will be able to . . .):

_____

_____

_____

_____

Rating of Importance (circle one):

   Nice   Important   Critical

Critical Vocabulary Words (Skill and Content):

Skill:

- _____
- _____
- _____

Content:

- _____
- _____
- _____

Standard and Number: _____

Skill in the Standard (students will be able to . . .):

_____

_____

_____

_____

Rating of Importance (circle one):

   Nice   Important   Critical

Critical Vocabulary Words (Skill and Content):

Skill:

- _____
- _____
- _____

Content:

- _____
- _____
- _____

Standard and Number: _____

Skill in the Standard (students will be able to . . .):

_____

_____

_____

_____

Rating of Importance (circle one):

   Nice   Important   Critical

Critical Vocabulary Words (Skill and Content):

Skill:

- _____
- _____
- _____

Content:

- _____
- _____
- _____

Team Essential Standards Guide

Team: _____ Year: _____

INSTRUCTIONAL PACING	ESSENTIAL STANDARD	ACADEMIC VOCABULARY	FORMATIVE FEEDBACK PROMPTS	LEARNING TARGETS AND MASTERY
Provide the month in which you will teach the essential standards and skills. *(Pacing guide)*	List the agreed-on essential standards and skills for the course or grade level. *(Those critical for all students)*	List the critical academic vocabulary that students will need to know. *(Vocabulary front-loaded prior to instruction)*	List formative feedback questions used to assess and provide feedback during instruction. *(Information-gathering prompts)*	List learning targets and describe what a proficient student will know and be able to do. *(Targets for all students)*

Source: Adapted from Buffum, A., & Mattos, M. (Eds.). (2015). It's about time: Planning interventions and extensions in secondary school. Bloomington, IN: Solution Tree Press.

Answering critical question one:

"What knowledge, skills, and dispositions should

every student acquire as a result of this unit,

this course, or this grade level?"

(DuFour et al., 2016, p. 36)

Gaining Shared Clarity and Defining Mastery

Whether your district has already identified the essential standards or your team has done the work, there is still work to complete. Effective teams go further by determining what the identified essential standards are asking students to know or demonstrate and what mastery looks like.

Shared clarity is when every teacher on a team understands, the same as the other teachers on the team, what a standard asks of students and the concepts and skills all students need to know or be able to do. In addition, having the same understanding of mastery may seem like a relatively simple task, but it tends to be one of the most demanding, requiring deep thought and discussions such as the following.

- "What is the standard asking the student to know and be able to do?"
- "Are there critical vocabulary terms related to instruction of the standard that students may struggle with?"
- "Are there consistent formative questions we can ask during instruction that will allow us to gather feedback regarding a student's progress?"
- "Are we able to identify and measure each target within the standard?"
- "Are we clear on what a student who has mastered the standard will know and be able to do with our content?"

Remember that identifying essential standards is only the first step to answering critical question one. A team may agree that a standard is essential, but unless there is shared agreement regarding what the standard says and what a student who has mastered it will know and be able to do, collaborative formative assessments begin to unravel, and collective intervention efforts become futile.

In *Simplifying the Journey*, the next step critical to a team's work and collective learning is to gain shared clarity and clearly define what mastery looks like. It's important to note that teachers who provide special education services possess unique expertise and insights into student learning. They should be part of the content collaborative team. Special educators should understand the essential standards as well as their content peers do so they can provide instruction that supports the unique needs of students who are entitled to an individualized education program (IEP). Further, including special educators as part of content collaborative teams enables them to contribute meaningfully to discussions about teaching, learning, and monitoring progress, ensuring that students who are IEP-entitled receive the necessary support to master grade-level standards. We are passionately convinced that this critical step is the key to team effectiveness, focused instruction, diagnostic assessment, and targeted intervention. Despite that, it is often overlooked.

In this chapter, you are guided through the process that teams engage in as they come to shared clarity and defined mastery for each essential standard. Gaining shared clarity on the essential standards and clearly defining what a student who has mastered them will know and be able to do helps teams focus on learning, and it inevitably leads to changes in instruction and assessment practices and increases teams' effectiveness.

Leading the Work— Specific Actions of School and Team Leaders

Leaders can take the following specific actions to clarify and communicate the work to be accomplished; support teachers as they learn together; monitor the work; and validate and celebrate teams as they learn to gain shared clarity and clearly define mastery.

Clarify and Communicate the Work

Once again, leaders must create a compelling case for teams to engage in the work of gaining clarity and defining mastery for each essential standard. Generally speaking, standards are ambiguously written with expectations of mastery and often vary greatly from teacher to teacher.

To understand a team's decisions, consider the following third-grade reading standard: "Ask and answer questions to demonstrate understanding of a text, referring explicitly to the text as the basis for the answers" (RL.3.1; National Governors Association Center for Best Practices & Council of Chief State School Officers, 2010). As teams gain shared clarity and define mastery for this standard, they must ask questions like these.

- "How many and what types of questions must a student ask and answer?"

- "What text or texts will we use to determine understanding of the text?"

- "What constitutes an *understanding* of the text?"

- "How will we assess this?"

Because of the ambiguity and resulting frequent misinterpretation, teams must have shared agreement regarding what mastery will look like for each essential standard. It's also important for the leader to consistently convey to teams that the work of identifying the essentials for each course and grade level is only the *first step* in the process.

To ensure that all students can master the essential standards, leaders need to engage in conversations addressing guiding questions with the team. These guiding questions may be as follows.

- "Does every team member understand what mastery looks like for each essential standard?"

- "Is your team able to quickly assess individual learning targets in a standard?"

- "How are you gathering information regarding students' progress and the impact of your practice during the unit of instruction?" (We go into greater detail about strategies for assessment in chapter 4, page 87, and chapter 5, page 115.)

Teams can gain shared clarity and define mastery by deeply discussing and agreeing on the following elements related to each essential standard.

- **Critical academic vocabulary:** Teams identify critical academic vocabulary that students will need to know to master the essential standard.

- **Formative feedback prompts:** Agreed-on formative feedback prompts serve as a verbal assessment that provides essential feedback to students about their progress toward mastery, and feedback regarding the effectiveness of a teacher's chosen teaching strategy. Formative assessments require an examination of rigor; Norman Webb's (1997) Depth of Knowledge (DOK) can help teams determine rigor, and the list of potential formative feedback prompts (page 77) has stems that can help.

- **Measurable learning targets:** At their very essence, standards are complex. Multiple skills or targets are embedded in standards. Clearly identifying these individual skills or targets will allow teams to quickly assess students' progress in each.

- **Defined mastery:** Along with being complex, standards are often written ambiguously. This requires teachers and teams to clearly define for the standards and skills that a student will know and be able to do in order to master each one.

Support Teachers as They Learn Together

Again, providing *time* for teacher teams to do this work is key for the leader. This step—gaining shared clarity and defining mastery—is *the* critical step that allows the team, and learning, to thrive. When teams can clearly define what mastery looks like, their instruction, assessment, and intervention practices can be more targeted. The challenge for leaders and teachers is that finding time for this work takes a lot of thought and creativity! Support for teachers in doing this work can come in various forms, including time, resources, and coaching.

How do leaders create time to do this work in an already-full schedule? Consider these ideas.

- Create common planning time in the master schedule.

- Have approved instructional support staff assist in classrooms to free teams up for a class period.

- Employ roving substitute teachers to cover classes.

- Use flexible or discretionary funds to pay teams that are willing to engage in the simplifying journey during off-contract time, such as summer vacation.

- Utilize other adults in the building to free a team from assembly duties or other supervision responsibilities and allow the team to work together.

Creating time for teams to engage in this valuable work is limited only by the leader's and the team's creativity.

As teams engage in this critical work, they will also benefit from coaching and additional resources that assist them in their collective learning. There are a myriad of resources in *Simplifying the Journey* to support them in their collective work. Again, we want to remind leaders that improving student learning begins with improving the behaviors and practices of the adults in the building.

Monitor the Work

Recognize that as teams learn together, they will often move through predictable stages of improvement. Table 2.1 explains the common stages that teams move through toward a shared understanding of mastery. Sharing this information with teachers can be helpful.

Table 2.1: Common Learning Stages for Teams in Understanding Mastery

STAGE 1: Minimal Understanding	STAGE 2: Developing	STAGE 3: Efficacy
Lack of awareness:	**Curricular priority:**	**Measurable targets:**
The team is unaware of the value that identifying essential standards and skills, gaining shared clarity, and defining mastery will have for student learning and team practices.	The team has carefully analyzed the standards and come to agreement on which are essential for students to know and be able to do.	For each essential standard, the team has identified clear learning targets that they can quickly measure through short formative assessments that are a seamless part of instruction.
Standard overload:	**Common vocabulary and formative feedback:**	**Defined mastery:**
The team is aware of the overwhelming number of standards and may see the value of prioritizing some, but spends time planning how to deliver all the standards.	The team has agreed on common vocabulary to load prior to instruction and has agreed on a few formative feedback questions to verbally ask during instruction.	The team has agreed on a shared description of mastery for each essential standard and on learning targets that clearly articulate the work that a student will know and be able to do to demonstrate mastery of the essential standards.

*Visit **go.SolutionTree.com/PLCbooks** for a free reproducible version of this table.*

For leaders, recognizing that teams will move through stages of development provides valuable information for monitoring and providing targeted coaching for the work. By using the criteria for each stage, teams can identify the stage that best describes where they are in the process, and they can identify the next stage of their development.

Validate and Celebrate Teams as They Learn

Can you imagine what it would feel like if you went to a football game and the only time the cheerleaders cheered was at the conclusion of the game? It would feel kind of weird, right? Whether a team leader or a school leader, you are undoubtedly the biggest team cheerleader. You are the head celebrator! With this responsibility, you will recognize, validate, and celebrate often. Much like cheerleaders, leaders consistently search for successes and small wins to recognize and validate as team members learn together. These celebrations will most likely serve as validation for the team that they're engaged in the right work. Don't wait until the end of the game to cheer!

It's important to note that validation and celebration are two distinct aspects of affirming the work of teachers and teams. *Validation* often involves acknowledging and recognizing a teacher's or team's thoughts and work. *Celebration* is a joyful expression recognizing the specific accomplishments of the teacher or team regarding this work. Both validation and celebration play important roles, and examples of each are in table 2.2.

Table 2.2: Validation and Celebration

VALIDATION	CELEBRATION
"Your work in identifying essential standards and clearly defining mastery has led to more targeted instruction."	"High five to you for using your collective expertise to identify essential standards and gain shared clarity for each. So we can celebrate your work and serve as a model for others, would you be willing to share your work and the thinking that went into this with our staff in the next faculty meeting?"
"Your emphasis and shared understanding of the essential standards showcases your commitment to ensuring all students achieve mastery in key areas of your content."	"Reviewing your students' assessment data has shown significant increases in their learning. Your collective work is paying off!"
"Your intentional focus on essential standards and gaining shared clarity for each not only benefits all students but also provides a cohesiveness from class to class."	"Kudos to you for your work in clearly defining mastery for each essential standard. This work is clearly evident in your classroom instruction and assessment practices. Let's celebrate. What's your favorite treat?"

Coaching the Work— Specific Actions of Learning Coaches

Shared clarity and defined mastery are an often missed—yet critical—step in the PLC process. Many teams are unaware of this step or skip it once they have agreed on essential skills. If teams fail to do this step, their collaborative formative assessments will begin to unravel into multiple articulated mastery levels, definitions, expectations, and outcomes— leading the interventions to become less targeted.

Consider This Scenario

> An elementary school mathematics team has spent a lot of time and effort deciding which standards are essential and has created team formative assessments for the first few units of study. The team has decided to

give a shared formative assessment on Wednesday of the coming week. Throughout the week, the team members focus their instruction on an identified essential standard and the associated skills. Teacher A realizes she will be unable to give the shared formative assessment on Wednesday because she took too much time on a skill and hasn't covered all the material in preparation for the shared formative assessment. Teachers B and C give the assessment on the agreed-on day. They wait for Teacher A to catch up before they review their data.

Eventually, the teachers meet as a team to discuss their results. Upon reviewing the results of their shared assessment, they discover that each teacher had different expectations of mastery. Along with this, the teachers all administered the assessment differently and provided varying degrees of support for the students. In studying their data, they also discover that they emphasized different parts of the essential standard during their instruction, and as a result, student learning as reflected on the shared formative assessment is inconsistent. As they review the results of this shared formative assessment, the question in each team member's mind is, "What went wrong?"

This team shows evidence of the following strengths.

- The team members share identification of essential standards, which deserves validation.

- They share a formative assessment.

- They use a pacing guide in an effort to cover material in a certain amount of time.

- They review the results together and are able to see some of the flaws in their execution.

Here are challenges the team members can work on to improve their efficiency and focus.

- Although they have agreed on essential standards, it is apparent the team members lack shared clarity regarding the essential standard being taught and collectively assessed.

- Their understanding of the essential standard being taught is limited to each teacher's own perspective. This lack of clarity became evident in the focus of their instruction and became further compounded in their shared assessment practices.

Coaching considerations for this team follow.

- **Coach teachers to shared gain understanding:** Encouraging teachers to gain shared understanding of the essential standards and skills will provide consistency in expectations from classroom to classroom.

- **Encourage teams to pace instruction together:** Two team members were able to meet the agreed-on date, while one team member was behind. To administer a shared formative assessment, team members need to pace their instruction similarly. Pacing together allows teams to assess together.

- **Agree on assessment practices:** Coaching the teachers to agree on the shared formative assessment and how the assessment will be administered will encourage consistency from classroom to classroom and provide data that are more accurate and meaningful.

Plan and Gather Evidence

Teams can participate in several practices to further develop shared clarity regarding each essential standard. For example, a team may take the shared formative assessment together prior to providing instruction for the unit. The team can then make necessary modifications to the shared formative assessment to alleviate misconceptions about expectations. Encourage the team to share and review individual lessons and strategies to help mitigate any problems and ensure that all students are learning the same information with consistent teacher expectations from classroom to classroom. As teams engage in this work, their conversations begin to focus on student learning and their professional learning.

To specifically engage in this step, perhaps a team knows working with a coach will benefit their work through this process. You may simply act as the scribe and information collector during those meetings after ensuring the team has the resources they need. You may also help keep the team on task according to the agenda and give your perspective should a disagreement arise. It is helpful for each team member to identify a goal they'd like to achieve during the team's collective work and share it with you before the meeting.

Ask teachers to remember the following as they work through the process.

- **This is collective learning.** The discussions are as valuable as the final product.

- **All teachers are to be equal parts of the process.** Their professional opinions are to be heard and honored.

To support teams, coaches can help schedule, review procedures, and ask clarifying questions before, during, and after this step. The steps for gaining shared clarity and defining mastery follow.

1. **Prior to the meeting, ensure that everyone on the team has a complete copy of the agenda.** Figure 2.1 is a partially completed example of the reproducible "Gaining Shared Clarity—Meeting Agenda" (page 56). You can see that this agenda lists further reproducible resources that the team members will use during their meeting: "Gaining Shared Clarity Cards" (page 57), "Teacher Team Workshop—Gaining Shared Clarity" (page 58), and "Gaining Shared Clarity" (page 61).

PEOPLE ATTENDING: Smith, Adams, and Vasquez	DATE: 9/13

TODAY'S TEAM GOALS:

1. Gain shared clarity on September's assessments
2. Gain shared clarity on October's assessments

MEETING NORMS:

1.
2.
3.
4.
5.

8:00–8:30 a.m.: Create meeting norms.

8:30 a.m.–2:00 p.m. (lunch around noon):

- Review September's and October's skills and common formative assessments.
    - ▷ What does mastery look like to each of us? We'll use the "Gaining Shared Clarity Cards" reproducible.
    - ▷ What does the team have in common in regard to the skills? We'll color-code when we complete the "Teacher Team Workshop—Gaining Shared Clarity" reproducible.
    - ▷ We'll define mastery based on the team's commonalities as we use the "Teacher Team Workshop—Gaining Shared Clarity" reproducible.
    - ▷ Collectively, we'll complete the "Gaining Shared Clarity" document.
- We'll repeat the preceding for each assessment we will give in September and October.

Figure 2.1: Gaining shared clarity—Meeting agenda example.

2. **Provide each team member one blank gaining shared clarity card (page 57) for each essential standard and skill being considered.** The team lead or facilitator (a coach or administrator) presents the first standard or skill. Without conversing, each team member writes an answer to the following question on their own card: What does mastery look like for this standard or skill?

    It's important that members *silently* consider and articulate their unique perspective regarding mastery. This silence is vital to the success of gaining shared clarity for three reasons: (1) it allows teachers time to think and formulate their own thoughts, (2) it stops any overbearing teachers from taking over the conversations, and (3) it allows more hesitant teachers to be heard. Each team member works independently to define mastery and prepares to contribute to conversations. Figure 2.2 is an example of one elementary teacher's card, and figure 2.3 (both page 44) is an example of one middle school teacher's card.

Without consulting your teammates, complete the following.

Skill:

ESS 3C: I can investigate the effect of materials in the path of a beam of light and emphasize how light can pass through objects or create shadows.

What does mastery look like for this standard or skill?

→ Use a light to show the effect on an object.

→ Identify if the object is illuminated, lit up, or see-through.

→ Explain why the object is affected by the light.

Source for standard: Nebraska State Board of Education, 2017.

Figure 2.2: Gaining shared clarity card, elementary example.

Without consulting your teammates, complete the following.

Skill:

5.NF.B.06: The extended students can "solve and create real-world problems in context involving multiplication of fractions and mixed numbers."

What does mastery look like for this standard or skill?

→ Multiply numbers.

→ Change a mixed number to an improper fraction.

→ Multiply the numerator.

→ Multiply the denominator.

→ Simplify.

→ Solve word problems.

→ Create a real-world example for a word problem.

Source for standard: Arizona Department of Education, 2018.

Figure 2.3: Gaining shared clarity card, middle school example.

---

3. **Collect all the gaining shared clarity cards.** These cards' authors can be anonymous if you prefer that. You can ensure that the respondents remain undisclosed by having members respond electronically prior to the meeting or hand in their responses beforehand. Begin completing the reproducible "Teacher Team Workshop—Gaining Shared Clarity" (page 58) on a presentation slide for the entire team to view. Review each card and transfer each unique perspective regarding mastery to the numbered teacher sections. Figure 2.4 is an elementary example, and figure 2.5 is a middle school example.

What does mastery look like for ESS 3C, "I can investigate the effect of materials in the path of a beam of light and emphasize how light can pass through objects or create shadows"?	
TEACHER 1	**TEACHER 2**
• Use a light to show the effect on an object. • Identify if the object is illuminated, lit up, or see-through. • Explain why the object is affected by the light.	• Place solid objects in front of light to create shadows. • Place clear objects in the path of light to show light passing through. • Discover different ways light can travel.
TEACHER 3	**TEACHER 4**
• Show how light changes on an object. • Explain how light cannot pass through an opaque object. • Explain how light can pass through a translucent object. • Determine what the materials are in objects that make them react to light in a certain way.	

Source for standard: Nebraska State Board of Education, 2017.

Figure 2.4: Teacher team workshop—Gaining shared clarity, elementary example.

What does mastery look like for 5.NF.B.06, "Solve and create real-world problems in context involving multiplication of fractions and mixed numbers"?	
TEACHER 1	**TEACHER 2**
• Multiply numbers. • Change a mixed number to an improper fraction. • Multiply the numerator. • Multiply the denominator. • Simplify. • Solve word problems. • Create a real-world example for a word problem.	• Convert a mixed number to a fraction greater than 1. • Multiply the numerator. • Multiply the denominator. • Simplify. (Convert the fraction back to a mixed number.) • Create a real-world problem. • Solve a real-world problem.

Source for standard: Arizona Department of Education, 2018.

Figure 2.5: Teacher team workshop—Gaining shared clarity, middle school example.

4. **After documenting all the mastery perspectives, everyone reviews them and you color-code them.** (Because the following examples cannot be color-coded, they will be starred, circled, and underlined instead.) For example,

if the skill being assessed is the investigation of how light affects different objects, highlight any mention of *use a light to show the effect on an object* in a specific color. Then highlight *identify if the object is illuminated, lit up, or see-through* in a different color. Keep doing this until you have labeled as much as possible. The different colors or symbols help the team conceptualize what the expectations are for the skill and whether the team wholly agrees or doesn't. Figure 2.6 is an elementary example, and figure 2.7 is a middle school example.

In figure 2.6, notice how the third teacher has a skill showing all three indicators (underlined, circled, and starred). This example team discussed how this would be a wonderful way to extend this skill. Students would be expected to articulate their rationales. In another example, a team might realize that some teachers forgot to list a skill and that it is mastery, not an extension.

What does mastery look like for ESS 3C, "I can investigate the effect of materials in the path of a beam of light and emphasize how light can pass through objects or create shadows"?

TEACHER 1	TEACHER 2
• <u>Use a light to show the effect on an object.</u>	• Place solid objects in front of light to create shadows. ★
• (Identify if the object is illuminated, lit up, or see-through.)	• (Place clear objects in the path of light to show light passing through.)
• Explain why the object is affected by the light. ★	• <u>Discover different ways light can travel.</u>

TEACHER 3	TEACHER 4
• <u>Show how light changes on an object.</u>	
• Explain how light cannot pass through an opaque object. ★	
• (Explain how light can pass through a translucent object.)	
• (<u>Determine what the materials are in objects that make them react to light in a certain way.</u> ★)	

Source for standard: Nebraska State Board of Education, 2017.

Figure 2.6: Teacher team workshop—Gaining shared clarity, coded elementary example.

What does mastery look like for 5.NF.B.06, "Solve and create real-world problems in context involving multiplication of fractions and mixed numbers"?

TEACHER 1	TEACHER 2
• ~~Multiply numbers.~~ • Change a mixed number to an improper fraction. • Multiply the numerator. ☆ • Multiply the denominator. • Simplify. • Solve word problems. ✗ • Create a real-world example for a word problem.	• Convert a mixed number to a fraction greater than 1. • Multiply the numerator. ☆ • Multiply the denominator. • Simplify. (Convert the fraction back to a mixed number.) • Create a real-world problem. • Solve a real-world problem. ✗

Source for standard: Arizona Department of Education, 2018.

Figure 2.7: Teacher team workshop—Gaining shared clarity, coded middle school example.

5. **Using the color-coded form, the team decides on what mastery looks like.** The elementary team completed the Mastered column and put the extension into the Extended column in figure 2.8. The middle school team has completed the Mastered column but hasn't yet completed any others, as shown in figure 2.9 (page 48).

Agreed-on mastery: Based on everyone's comments, what does mastery (level 3) look like?

4—EXTENDED	3—MASTERED	2—APPROACHING	1—SUPPORTED
I can determine what the materials are in objects that make them react to light in certain ways.	I can discover different ways light can affect an object. I can place an object in front of the light to create shadows. I can place an object in front of the light to show illumination, or clarity.		

Source for standard: Nebraska State Board of Education, 2017.

Figure 2.8: Example elementary teacher team workshop—Gaining shared clarity.

Agreed-on mastery: Based on everyone's comments, what does mastery (level 3) look like?			
4—EXTENDED	3—MASTERED	2—APPROACHING	1—SUPPORTED
	I can restate and answer the question (topic sentence). I can use appropriate transitions. I can correctly cite two pieces of relevant evidence. I can provide an analysis for each piece of relevant evidence. I can provide a concluding sentence.		

Source for standard: Utah State Office of Education, 2013.

Figure 2.9: Example middle school teacher team workshop—Gaining shared clarity.

6. **The team completes the "Gaining Shared Clarity" document (page 61).** It can help to have a slide deck with the customizable document on each slide. Have one slide for every essential standard and skill the team is evaluating. This document separates four areas of focus: (1) mastery, (2) measurable learning targets, (3) critical academic vocabulary, and (4) formative feedback prompts. These areas support shared clarity and contribute to student learning by setting clear expectations that the entire team understands and agrees on. For example, all the teachers can ask the same specific questions and gauge student mastery. They also have common vocabulary that helps when the team begins to intervene and share students. Having common vocabulary across the team helps maintain equity for students and helps their learning grow because they understand what any teacher is asking. For elementary and middle school examples, see figure 2.10 and figure 2.11 (page 50). The team repeats this process for each essential standard they've identified.

ESSENTIAL STANDARD:

1-PS4-3: "Plan and conduct investigations to determine the effect of placing objects made with different materials in the path of a beam of light."

LIST MEASURABLE LEARNING TARGETS.

I can place different objects and explain the effects of light on the objects.

DEFINE *MASTERY.*

(Define what a student who has mastered the standard will be able to do with the content. These statements should be written in student-friendly language. I can statements are helpful for students to see what they are going to be able to do.)

1. I can discover different ways light can affect an object.
2. I can place an object in front of the light to create shadows.
3. I can place an object in front of the light to show illumination, or clarity.

PRIOR TO UNIT OF INSTRUCTION	DURING UNIT OF INSTRUCTION
Critical Academic Vocabulary	Formative Prompts
(Vocabulary front-loaded prior to instruction)	*(Feedback for student learning and teaching practices)*
<ul><li>Investigate</li><li>Emphasize</li><li>Materials</li><li>Light</li><li>Reflect</li><li>Travel</li><li>Shadows</li><li>Clear</li></ul>	Can you explain how _____ affected _____? Can you formulate a theory for _____?

Source for standard: Next Generation Science Standards, 2013.

Figure 2.10: Gaining shared clarity, elementary example.

ESSENTIAL STANDARD:

5.NF.B.06. Students can "solve and create real-world problems in context involving multiplication of fractions and mixed numbers."

LIST MEASURABLE LEARNING TARGETS.

I can solve real-world problems by multiplying fractions and mixed numbers.

DEFINE *MASTERY*.

(Define what a student who has mastered the standard will be able to do with the content. These statements should be written in student-friendly language. I can statements are helpful for students to see what they are going to be able to do.)

1. I can convert a mixed number to a fraction greater than 1.
2. I can convert a fraction greater than 1 to a mixed number.
3. I can simplify a fraction by finding the greatest common factor.
4. I can multiply the numerator.
5. I can multiply the denominator.
6. I can use fraction skills to solve word problems.

PRIOR TO UNIT OF INSTRUCTION	DURING UNIT OF INSTRUCTION
Critical Academic Vocabulary	**Formative Prompts**
(Vocabulary front-loaded prior to instruction)	*(Feedback for student learning and teaching practices)*
• Numerator • Denominator • Mixed number • Greatest common factor (GCF) • Simplify • Product • Equation • Convert fraction greater than 1 • Solve • Real world	$\frac{3}{4}$: Box the numerator and circle the denominator. $\frac{6}{24}$: Find the GCF and simplify. $5\frac{1}{4}$: Convert to a fraction greater than 1. $\frac{24}{3}$: Convert to a mixed number and simplify. **Solve:** $\frac{3}{4} \times \frac{2}{3} =$ _____. **Solve:** $2\frac{1}{3} \times 3\frac{1}{4} =$ _____. Donny has $5\frac{1}{2}$ pieces of ribbon that each measure $2\frac{1}{4}$ inches. Write and solve an equation that shows the total length of ribbon.

Source for standard: Arizona Department of Education, 2018.

Figure 2.11: Gaining shared clarity, middle school example.

You can see in figure 2.12 that the middle school mathematics team began with the Mastered column and then worked its way through the rest of the rubric.

Learning Target: 5.NF.B.06. Students can "solve and create real-world problems in context involving multiplication of fractions and mixed numbers."			
1—SUPPORTED	**2—FOUNDATIONAL**	**3—MASTERED**	**4—ADVANCED**
• Needs one-on-one support to convert a mixed number to a fraction greater than 1 • Needs one-on-one support to convert a fraction greater than 1 to a mixed number • Needs one-on-one support to simplify a fraction by finding the greatest common factor (GCF) • Needs one-on-one support to multiply multi-digit numbers • Needs one-on-one support or charts to know mathematics facts • Needs one-on-one support to interpret word problems	• Is unclear about the process to convert a mixed number to a fraction greater than 1 (such as missing steps) • Is unclear about the process to convert a fraction greater than 1 to a mixed number (such as fractions as division) • Is unclear about number sense (such as division, prime numbers, or composite numbers) • Is unclear about multi-digit multiplication • Is unclear on mathematics facts • Is unclear on interpreting word problems	• Can convert a mixed number to a fraction greater than 1 • Can convert a fraction greater than 1 to a mixed number • Can simplify a fraction by finding the GCF • Can multiply the numerator • Can multiply the denominator • Can use fraction skills to solve word problems	• Can create a real-world problem • Can solve multistep word problems

Source for standard: Arizona Department of Education, 2018.
Source: © 2022 by Talore Miller. Used with permission.
Figure 2.12: Learning targets, middle school example.

After gaining shared clarity and defining mastery, the team completes the "Team Essential Standards Guide" (page 33), examples of which are in figure 2.13 (page 52) and figure 2.14 (page 53). These are continuations and more complete versions of the example in figure 1.5 (page 25).

Team: First grade (science essential standards)			**Year:** 2024	
INSTRUCTIONAL PACING	**ESSENTIAL STANDARD**	**ACADEMIC VOCABULARY**	**FORMATIVE FEEDBACK PROMPTS**	**LEARNING TARGETS AND MASTERY**
Provide the month in which you will teach the essential standards and skills. *(Pacing guide)*	List the agreed-on essential standards and skills for the course or grade level (created from the standards required of teachers). *(Those critical for all students)*	List the critical academic vocabulary that students will need to know. *(Vocabulary front-loaded prior to instruction)*	List formative feedback questions used to assess and provide feedback during instruction. *(Information-gathering prompts)*	List learning targets and describe what a proficient student will know and be able to do. *(Targets for all students)*
August (First Week)	**ESS 3A:** I can investigate to show the cause-and-effect relationship between sound and vibrating matter.			
August (Second Week)	**ESS 3B:** I can use a model to show the effect of light on objects to either illuminate them or give their own light off.			
August (Third Week)	**ESS 3C:** I can investigate the effect of materials in the path of a beam of light and emphasize how light can pass through objects or create shadows.	• Investigate • Emphasize • Materials • Light • Reflect • Travel • Shadows • Clear	Can you explain how _____ affected _____? Can you formulate a theory for _____?	I can discover different ways light can affect an object. I can place an object in front of the light to create shadows. I can place an object in front of the light to show illumination, or clarity.
August— September (Fourth Week / First Week)	**ESS 3D:** I can design a device that uses light or sound to solve communicating over a long distance.			

Source for standard: Nebraska State Board of Education, 2017.

Figure 2.13: Team essential standards guide, elementary example.

Team: Fifth-grade mathematics (5.NF.B.06: Highly proficient students can "solve and create real-world problems in context involving multiplication of fractions and mixed numbers.")			Year: 2024	
INSTRUCTIONAL PACING	**ESSENTIAL STANDARD**	**ACADEMIC VOCABULARY**	**FORMATIVE FEEDBACK PROMPTS**	**LEARNING TARGETS AND MASTERY**
Provide the month in which you will teach the essential standards and skills. *(Pacing guide)*	List the agreed-on essential standards and skills for the course or grade level. *(Those critical for all students)*	List the critical academic vocabulary that students will need to know. *(Vocabulary front-loaded prior to instruction)*	List formative feedback questions used to assess and provide feedback during instruction. *(Information-gathering prompts)*	List learning targets and describe what a proficient student will know and be able to do. *(Targets for all students)*
August (First Week)	**5.NF.B.06:** Students can "solve and create real-world problems in context involving multiplication of fractions and mixed numbers."	• Mixed number • Greatest common factor (GCF) • Simplify • Product • Equation • Convert fraction greater than 1	$\frac{3}{4}$: Box the numerator and circle the denominator. $\frac{6}{24}$: Find the greatest common factor and simplify. $5\frac{1}{4}$: Convert to a fraction greater than 1. $\frac{24}{3}$: Convert to a mixed number and simplify.	I can convert a mixed number to a fraction greater than 1. I can convert a fraction greater than 1 to a mixed number. I can simplify a fraction by finding the greatest common factor.
August (Second Week)	**5.NF.B.06:** Students can "solve and create real-world problems in context involving multiplication of fractions and mixed numbers."	• Numerator • Denominator • Solve • Real world	**Solve:** $\frac{3}{4} \times \frac{2}{3} =$ _____ **Solve:** $2\frac{1}{3} \times 3\frac{1}{4} =$ _____. Donny has $5\frac{1}{2}$ pieces of ribbon that each measure $2\frac{1}{4}$ inches. Write and solve an equation that shows the total length of ribbon.	I can multiply the numerator. I can multiply the denominator. I can use fraction skills to solve word problems.

Source for standard: Arizona Department of Education, 2018.

Figure 2.14: Team essential standards guide, middle school example.

The question bank for coaches in figure 2.15 helps you guide teams as they come to agreement on learning outcomes expected of all students.

What is each teacher doing in the classroom?	Is the pacing guide viable for all teachers?
What are students doing in the classroom?	What will students be doing to show that they have reached mastery?
What is important background knowledge that all students need to be successful?	Can each teacher articulate the expectation for mastery?
Have all teachers reached a common understanding regarding the essential skills?	Can students articulate the expectation for mastery?
Have new teachers (whether new to teaching or new to the team) gained the same clarity as veteran teachers?	What are some quick formative prompts to determine where students are in their learning?

Figure 2.15: Question bank—Shared clarity and defined mastery.

Reflect to Elicit Change

Ask the team to reflect on what they have learned from completing the activity together. Celebrate the wins, shore up the weaknesses, and adjust what didn't work. There should be plenty of validation and celebration along the way, while collective learning continues. By doing this, teachers and teams can avoid the one behavior that will limit a team's growth: complacency. The entire school needs to be part of this work. Part of the reflection should include how to get the required support. That support can come from many different people on the staff, from secretaries to counselors to instructional aides to special education teachers.

It is through the intentionality of their work, combined with a focus on shared clarity and defined mastery, that educators can ultimately create the conditions for student and adult learning to flourish; see figure 2.16.

		START	STOP	CONTINUE
ACTION TWO: SHARED CLARITY AND DEFINED MASTERY		Taking tests together before the unit to align how we will teach and what will be taught to get on the same page	Leaving teachers behind or pushing ahead without the team	Using common formative assessments that we have developed
SMART Goal		Use team time to take each common formative assessment the week before we start a unit; discuss expectations and results and how they apply to student learning.		
Reflection		Wow! Taking tests together really allowed our team to understand the differences we each have when interpreting the meaning of a skill. We caught potential problems before they occurred with our students. We are definitely continuing this practice because it helps align our classes and also works as a review for upcoming material.		

Figure 2.16: Example of team coaching inventory, action two.

Don't Miss This

Be aware of the following things while leading and coaching the journey.

- **Gaining shared clarity and defined mastery is the key *Simplifying the Journey* action in the collective work:** Although this action will require an initial investment of time and effort, the payoff is evident in the students' learning and the team's efficacy.

- **Revisit this action prior to and at the conclusion of each unit as well as at the end of each year:** This is especially important as new teachers are added to the team. With each new year, and each new teacher added to a team, fresh, valuable perspectives will add to the work of the team.

- **It's important to commit to learning together:** As team members understand the unique perspectives and experiences of everyone on the team, and they remain vulnerable and willing to learn, ideas take hold and adult learning flourishes.

- **Include support staff in your collaborative work:** Special educators and instructional aides are valuable parts of a team, as each can offer unique perspectives and specialized skills as your team gains shared clarity while adding valuable insight to the scaffolding necessary for all learners to flourish.

Gaining Shared Clarity—Meeting Agenda

People Attending:	Date:

TODAY'S TEAM GOALS:

1.
2.
3.
4.
5.

MEETING NORMS:

1.
2.
3.
4.
5.

_____–_____ (time span):

_____–_____ (time span):

Simplifying the Journey © 2024 Solution Tree Press • SolutionTree.com

Visit **go.SolutionTree.com/PLCbooks** to download this free reproducible.

Gaining Shared Clarity Cards

Without consulting your teammates, complete the following.

Skill: _____

_____

What does mastery look like for this standard or skill?

- _____
- _____
- _____
- _____
- _____

Without consulting your teammates, complete the following.

Skill: _____

_____

What does mastery look like for this standard or skill?

- _____
- _____
- _____
- _____
- _____

Without consulting your teammates, complete the following.

Skill: _____

_____

What does mastery look like for this standard or skill?

- _____
- _____
- _____
- _____
- _____

Teacher Team Workshop—Gaining Shared Clarity

What does mastery look like for this standard or skill?

ESSENTIAL STANDARD AND SKILL:

TEACHER 1	TEACHER 2

TEACHER 3	TEACHER 4

AGREED-ON MASTERY: BASED ON EVERYONE'S COMMENTS, WHAT DOES MASTERY (LEVEL 3) LOOK LIKE?

EXTENDED	MASTERED	APPROACHING	SUPPORTED

Gaining Shared Clarity

ESSENTIAL STANDARD:

LIST MEASURABLE LEARNING TARGETS.

1. _____
2. _____
3. _____

DEFINE *MASTERY*.

(Define what a student who has mastered the standard will be able to do with the content. These statements should be written in student-friendly language. I can statements are helpful for students to see what they are going to be able to do.)

1. _____
2. _____
3. _____
4. _____
5. _____
6. _____

PRIOR TO UNIT OF INSTRUCTION	DURING UNIT OF INSTRUCTION
Critical Academic Vocabulary	**Formative Prompts**
(Vocabulary front-loaded prior to instruction)	*(Feedback for student learning and teaching practices)*

Answering critical question two:

"How will we know when each student has

acquired the essential knowledge and skills?"

(DuFour et al., 2016, p. 36)

Encouraging Student Ownership Through Student Self-Assessment

Students are often unfamiliar with their learning destinations. As a result, instruction may seem ambiguous or lacking in logical connections between what a teacher is teaching and what the teacher expects of students as they master the standard. To facilitate learning, students need clear, attainable steps in the learning process and clear learning outcomes. Further, they need to be able to assess their own learning, since "deeper learning is enhanced when formative assessment is used to . . . involve students in self- and peer assessment" (Pellegrino & Hilton, 2012, p. 166). This can be the difference between a student's educational success and endless frustration.

The next step in *Simplifying the Journey* focuses on creating student ownership by providing opportunities to self-assess. As teams clearly articulate what mastery looks like for each essential standard and learning target, they can share this with the students, helping them become active parts of their learning journey.

Leading the Work—
Specific Actions of School and Team Leaders

Leaders can take the following specific actions to clarify and communicate the work to be accomplished; support teachers as they learn together; monitor the work; and validate and celebrate teams as they learn to help students take ownership via self-assessment.

Clarify and Communicate the Work

Emphasize that learning in the classroom follows a pattern. Call on teachers to design learning progressions as part of their team's practices. In the previous chapter, we shared the importance of gaining shared clarity and clearly defining what mastery looks like for each essential standard and learning target. When teams gain a shared understanding of what all students must know and be able to do, and then clearly articulate what that looks like, this becomes a launching pad into student self-assessment. Self-assessment nurtures a profound sense of responsibility in students for their own education. Instead of passively taking part in a lesson, students can actively engage as they measure their own learning progress against exemplary work and recognizing strengths and areas for improvement. It also can result in a sense of satisfaction as students work toward mastery. Furthermore, the ability to self-assess is a critical life skill that nurtures increased confidence, resilience, and continuous improvement—all essential outside the classroom.

Support Teachers as They Learn Together

As this could be new thinking for teams, leaders must continually provide support for teachers and teams as they design and implement learning progressions in the classroom. This support may include the following.

- **Time to do the work:** As with all the work required to successfully work in collaboration, time outside classrooms is required. Leaders can provide time to do the work through creatively finding time for teachers. This may include hiring substitute teachers for the day, creating common prep periods for teams, or covering a team's classes with administration, counselors, or other certified school personnel for a period or more.

- **Resources:** Begin by asking teachers what resources they need to assist in their work. Common responses may include books related to the subject, video resources, or attendance at trainings or conferences that focus on this work.

- **Coaching:** Support through coaching is critical as teams rethink assessment and learn more about student learning progressions. You learn more about how to coach this action next.

Monitor the Work

Leaders can monitor the critical action of student self-assessment and ownership by frequently attending classes and asking students the following questions. Share these questions with teachers with the encouragement to consistently ask the questions of students as part of the learning process.

- **"What are you learning?"** Students should be able to articulate what it is they're *learning*, such as identifying the theme of the novel they're reading, and not what it is they're *doing*, such as filling out a worksheet.

- **"How will you know if you've learned it?"** Students should be able to describe what they will be able to do when they have mastered the standard or skill. This moves students away from representing learning in the form of a percentage ("I got 67 percent") and toward describing what they will be able to do.

- **"What do you plan to do when you get stuck while you learn?"** In learning anything new, there will be times of accelerated learning and times of productive struggle. A just-right productive struggle is an integral part of the learning process that should be consistently communicated to students throughout the learning experience. Encouraging students to have strategies for when they get stuck helps them prepare for the inevitable challenges that come as part of the learning process, and it builds resilience in students.

As students provide answers to these questions, they provide the leader insight into not only the students' learning but also critical feedback regarding learning progressions in the classroom.

Validate and Celebrate Teams as They Learn

As with any step in this journey, recognizing the work of teams and the steps they take is critical to their collective learning. Share team-created examples of student progressions with other staff members, provide opportunities for teams to share their work, and possibly record a two-minute video segment of them explaining their learning progressions to be shared with staff; these are all ways to validate and celebrate the work of teams. (High fives and a favorite treat never hurt either!)

Coaching the Work—Specific Actions of Learning Coaches

According to John Hattie's 2018 updated list of factors related to student achievement, self-reported grades rank second, with an effect size of 1.33 (Waack, 2018). Student self-assessment and ownership are some of the most exciting parts of this simplified process because many elements of it include what is happening in the classroom and how the students are reacting to it. For example, teachers provide checklists or graphic organizers where students can use a check mark to indicate when they have achieved a learning target, or students ask the teacher to stamp or put a sticker on a bubble sheet when they have achieved specific targets. Use your ingenuity to develop a system that works for you, your team, and your students. This encourages much-needed student engagement in the classroom.

Consider This Scenario

A middle school physical education team is completing a unit on soccer. They expect the unit to last approximately two weeks. The team members are clear about what they expect for mastery, and they have articulated the criteria through

> a clearly designed rubric, chunked the individual skills, and taught different skills and levels throughout the unit. Because of the need to get to the next unit before the weather gets bad, the team takes very little time to assess learning along the way; after all, the students are playing games almost every day.
>
> At the end of the two-week unit, each student demonstrates for their teacher the stated skills. Unfortunately, because of the sheer number of students to evaluate, no one receives feedback on their skills for nearly a month. As a result, instruction has already begun on the next unit. When students finally get their skills assessments, the feedback is mostly irrelevant because the students are simply interested in passing the unit. Their attention has turned to the next unit, which the teachers are hurrying through. Unfortunately, the teachers are also burned-out because of the time it took to grade every student on soccer skills.

The strengths of the team in the preceding scenario are as follows.

- The team is clear with their expectations of mastery and has developed targeted rubrics to help evaluate and encourage student self-assessment.

- There is evidence that the teachers are working together as a team.

- The team has taken a complex task (playing soccer) and chunked the individual skills into smaller parts.

A coach or facilitator can assist the team with these areas of challenge.

- **Overwhelmed teachers:** The teachers took on the role of "evaluator," and the students only had to comply, not actively learn. The teachers provided feedback, but it was delayed because of their limited time and overwhelming workload, negating the impact of provided feedback on student learning.

- **Student involvement in evaluating learning:** A very detailed rubric was provided, but little, if any, immediate feedback was provided. The students were never asked to evaluate their own skills or articulate those skills until the final assessment. By the time the feedback arrived, students had moved on to the next unit of instruction.

Coaching considerations for this team follow.

- **Have students help with feedback:** Hattie assigns self-reported grades an effect size of 1.33 (Waack, 2018). Students can be in charge of their own learning by explaining where they have been, why they are at a certain place in the learning progression, and what they need to do to move forward. Teachers can learn a lot about a student with this information. Feedback from students to the teacher is the most effective form (Waack, 2018). Develop some ways that involve students' explaining their personal learning journeys.

- **Provide feedback in a timely manner:** Give students the actionable information as soon as possible.

Plan and Gather Evidence

Coaches can help teams work on engaging students in ways that encourage the students to take ownership of their learning and become involved in self-assessment.

STUDENT OWNERSHIP

Some suggestions to involve students in their own learning follow. As a coach, choose one of the following and set specific goals (or come up with your own strategy and set goals around it). Remember that being intentional about our actions increases not only our abilities as educators but also students' learning. List the targets to be reached throughout the unit, and consider the following: How can students track their own learning? Is there a specific system in place? Have you instructed students on how to do this, and have they practiced using the method? How will students receive feedback? Help teachers clearly express how this will look in their classrooms and across teams.

- **Centers to practice specific skills:** Coach teams to chunk the skills of a learning target or standard into specific parts. In the scenario earlier in this chapter (page 65), for example, the physical education coaches would have centers set up for dribbling left and right, passing, kicking, receiving, reviewing the field setup, and following rules of play. The centers example in figure 3.1 (page 68) is for middle school science skills practice. Students choose one of the four tasks listed. These centers can be physically separated around a room at individual desks, or they can even be separated digitally. The key is that students are provided specific guidelines to assess themselves so they can attend the learning stations that are relevant to their learning—either intervention or extension activities.

- **Student choice menus:** Letting students choose how to show mastery creates in them ownership of their learning. Along with ownership, offering choices in extended learning opportunities provides variety after students have grasped the standard or skill. Figure 3.2 (page 69) is an example of a student choice menu. Notice, for task three, what the students are being asked to do. This team has separated tasks on their assignment so that students can identify what task they still need to learn and they can go to just that station. The differences between centers and student choice menus will be the number of offerings and the physical setup. Centers have students moving to different spots (in the room or online) where they perform different skills. Most classrooms can allow up to five centers at a time. In contrast, student choice menus allow a wider variety of offerings. Student choice menus most often offer students a medium or a communication style that best suits their needs, allowing a much more individualized learning experience.

LEARNING TARGET:

I can develop and use a model to describe the cycling of matter and flow of energy among living and nonliving parts in an ecosystem.

TASK ONE:	**TASK TWO:**
Using the following words, write the organisms in the correct locations on the food chain.	Match each term with its correct definition.

Fox | Grass | Rabbit | Cougar

Producers — Organisms that break down dead waste and recycle matter

Consumers — Organisms that make their own food

Decomposers — Organisms that eat other organisms

TASK THREE:	**TASK FOUR:**
A food web is a more accurate model to show the flow of energy in an ecosystem because:	Match the energy level to its correct location on the energy (trophic) pyramid.

More energy

Less energy

1 – MINIMAL	2 – APPROACHING	3—MASTERED	Teacher Feedback:
I am at the beginning of learning this. I have many questions and I am not sure what to do most of the time.	I am still learning this. I still have some questions and am unsure sometimes.	I feel like I know this pretty well. I get almost every task right the first time.	3—Mastered 2—Approaching 1—Minimal

Source: © 2022 by Teri Pay, Kengie Gass, & Amy Hunt. Used with permission.

Figure 3.1: Centers example, middle school science.

LEARNING TARGET:

I can plan and carry out an investigation by <u>adding</u> or <u>removing</u> heat energy and explain its effect on matter as well as design an object, tool, or process to <u>minimize</u> or <u>maximize</u> heat energy transfer.

TASK ONE:	**TASK TWO:**
What is the flow of energy in the following example?	**Label the following images based on the type of heat transfer shown.**

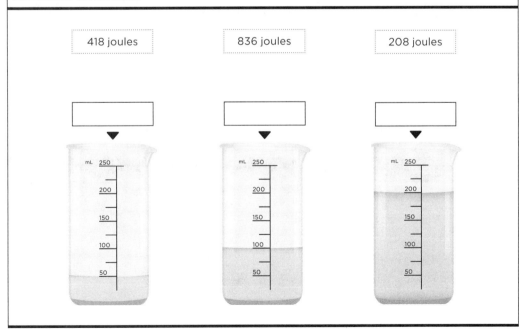

TASK ONE (continued)

a. The energy is flowing from the ice to the hand.

b. The energy is flowing from the hand to the ice.

TASK TWO (continued)

Conduction	Convection	Radiation

TASK THREE:

Investigate the heat capacities of different samples of water. Measure the amount of energy, in joules, needed to raise the temperature of the water in three different beakers. Predict the amount of heat energy needed to heat the water by <u>drawing a line from the amount to the appropriate beaker.</u>

418 joules	836 joules	208 joules

Figure 3.2: Example student choice menu with different tasks.

Extensions are often an afterthought, but they are important for the students who already understand. Extensions help those particular students grow by challenging them. Extensions work three ways: (1) they help someone gain a deeper understanding of a skill, (2) they help someone gain a broader understanding of a skill, or (3) they help someone gain a higher-level understanding of a skill. Providing extensions for these students addresses the fourth critical question.

Depending on the academic calendar, students can pick one extension to focus on each trimester or semester and then one of the yearlong extensions to focus on as well. The menu in figure 3.3 can work in many different ways for grades K–12. Depending on the student's skills and grade level, the extensions can be changed and edited to fit.

TRIMESTER ONE

- Elks Lodge essay
- ABC book about S. E. Hinton's *The Outsiders* (done as a pair)
- Movie script for *The Outsiders*
- Movie poster for *The Outsiders* (to include five elements of literature)
- Service project helping collect gifts for orphans
- Peer tutoring
- Newbery book
- Contest book
- Slideshow about a poet

TRIMESTER TWO

- Shakespeare festival
- Letter to a hero
- Service project gathering care packages for refugees
- ABC book about refugees (done as a pair)
- Investigation about survivors of a life-threatening situation (If possible, interview someone who is willing to share their story. Identify the characteristics that person shares with characters you have read about in survival books.)

TRIMESTER THREE

- Argumentative essay to the principal
- Argumentative essay presentation
- Youth creative-writing contest
- ABC book about wild birds (done as a pair)
- Service project creating May Day baskets for the elderly
- Research on survival techniques used in a specific wilderness area in summer or winter (Suggest and describe in detail an inventive technique that might be used in that same type of area.)
- Written and illustrated story
- Essay (for example, a spring break or most memorable birthday narrative)

ALL-YEAR EXTENSIONS

- Photo album for one of the characters in the novel with descriptive comments under each photograph describing the scene
- Newsela article
- Infographic
- Historical fiction and a report on the actual event
- Science fiction book (Talk about the science that we don't have.)
- Author study (Read a book and learn about the author; then report on the author rather than the book.)
- Peer tutoring
- Artistic representation of a scene in a novel
- Genre study
- Board game for your book (Ideas include crossword puzzles and quizzes.)

Source: © 2022 by Maren Powers & Amy Greene. Used with permission.

Figure 3.3: Example student choice menu with different English language arts extensions.

Consider the following student choices.

- **High-low comparison:** Students get examples of what teachers expect, rank their mastery using a rubric, and explain why they ranked the work a certain way. You might ask teachers what targets their students are trying to reach and suggest they add those targets to a checklist of items for students to use as a reference. See figure 3.4 (page 72) for an example. Then, you could ask, "How can students' reactions to the checklist inform instruction?" Next, with the teachers, determine some common problems that have occurred in the past. Create a sample that highlights some of those problems to help foster introspection and growth.

- **Graphic organizers:** Graphic organizers can list expectations for students to check their work themselves, review with a teacher, or get feedback from another student or the teacher when they feel they have reached the stated mastery. See figure 3.5 (page 73) for an example. Graphic organizers work well for visual learners. Many students appreciate a visual affirmation of their learning and those items that are still deficits. The example shows how a teacher can stamp a target on mastery but also leave feedback for students to continue learning. That feedback helps the student work independently and reveals to the teacher what skills might need reteaching. The slide numbers give another layer of specificity to help students take charge of their own learning. When a student gains mastery, the feedback comment can be crossed out. Coaches can help develop or gather evidence of effectiveness.

PROMPT:

Create a professional presentation using credible sources and relevant evidence explaining struggles, successes, and reasons for a specific group to settle in Utah.

- ☐ We can state the topic with a clarifying subtitle.
- ☐ We can create an organized, readable poster.
- ☐ We can determine and correctly cite at least three important facts (quoted and paraphrased).
- ☐ We can analyze why the facts are relevant to immigration.
- ☐ We can include at least one relevant image correctly cited with a descriptor and in-text citation.
- ☐ We can write a conclusion with a specific real-world message.
- ☐ We have produced an error-free works cited page.
- ☐ We have consistently used correct punctuation, capitalization, and spelling.

Is this poster showing mastery based on the prompt and the preceding criteria? (Did you check all of the boxes?)

What needs to change in order for it to show mastery? If you did not check all of the boxes, what are the specific skills that need to be relearned, or what needs to be fixed?

Source: © 2022 by Sheline Miller & Amy Mangelson. Used with permission.

Figure 3.4: High-low example.

Name: Shane	**Class Period:** 2

RESEARCH: GLOBAL EVENTS			
Process		**Content**	
Independently, I can create a slide presentation explaining the historical significance of a major historical event.		Independently, I can use primary sources and/or oral histories to analyze the impact of a national or global event (World War I, the Spanish flu pandemic, the Great Depression, World War II, or the Japanese American internment), or on an individual or community in Utah (standard 3.2).	
☐ Slide 8	☐ Slide 9	☐ Slide 10	☐ Slide 11
Practice	**Practice**	**Practice**	**Evidence of Learning**
Independently, I can read and annotate a text to find facts to analyze the impact of national or global events on Utah. YEAH!	Independently, I can find and correctly cite a relevant picture. YEAH!	Independently, I can write a conclusion with a real-world message. YEAH!	Independently, I can use critical research skills to create a slide presentation. YEAH!
☐	☐	☐	3 2 1
☐ Slides 14, 15, 16, 17	☐ Slide 18		☐ Slides 20, 21, 22, 23
Practice	**Evidence of Learning**		
Independently, I can learn from others about the impact of a national or global event on Utah. YEAH!	Independently, I can critically analyze facts to succinctly respond to a prompt about global events impacting Utah (standard 3.2). YEAH!		I can extend my learning by completing the extension on COVID-19 in Utah. Look at your transitions and capitalization. 4
☐	3 2 1		

AM I PROFICIENT IN *ALL* MY WORK?	Circle one. Yes No

If no, what steps will I take to reach mastery?

Source for standard: Utah State Office of Education, 2013.

Figure 3.5: Graphic organizer example.

- **Goal setting:** This occurs at the beginning of each unit, when students assess where they are and where they perceive themselves being at the end of the unit. See figure 3.6 for an example of a student's goal setting. The light gray is where the student thought he was at the start of the unit, and the dark gray is where he thought he was at the end of the unit. The student's actual level of understanding per the teacher is circled.

PROCESS:

I can strengthen my reading skills by using a problem-solution graphic organizer to comprehend human interdependence.

Rate your level of understanding now and where you want to be at the end of the unit.

4	3	2	1	Earned
				③

CONTENT:

I can describe the effects of events, movements, and innovations (such as the organized labor movement and the Great Depression) on Utah's economic development (standard 3.3).

Rate your level of understanding now and where you want to be at the end of the unit.

4	3	2	1	Earned
				③

Source for standard: Utah State Office of Education, 2013.
Source: © 2022 by Sheline Miller & Amy Mangelson. Used with permission.

Figure 3.6: Goal-setting example.

- **Digital experiences to differentiate and individualize learning:** Teams can choose what they have available through their district and their own experiences. Some examples could be the use of tools such as Kahoot!, Pear Deck, or interactive documents that send the learner to different places based on answers or exploration, and the use of recordings. Digital resources are nearly endless.

SELF-ASSESSMENT

Student self-assessment is a concept that many teachers see the value in but find diffi-cult to implement. As a coach, if you focus on the teacher actions in figure 3.7, that will inherently affect a student's ability to take ownership over learning.

The following sections take coaches through what steps they can guide teachers through as they enable student ownership via self-assessment.

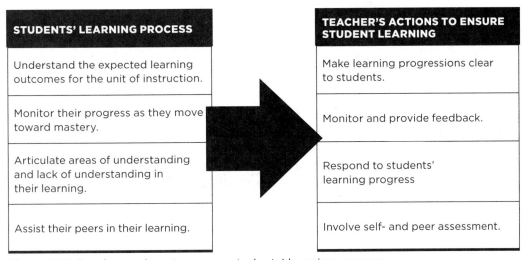

STUDENTS' LEARNING PROCESS	TEACHER'S ACTIONS TO ENSURE STUDENT LEARNING
Understand the expected learning outcomes for the unit of instruction.	Make learning progressions clear to students.
Monitor their progress as they move toward mastery.	Monitor and provide feedback.
Articulate areas of understanding and lack of understanding in their learning.	Respond to students' learning progress
Assist their peers in their learning.	Involve self- and peer assessment.

Figure 3.7: Teacher actions to ensure students' learning process.

Step 1: Make Learning Progressions Clear to Students

For students to understand the expected learning outcomes for a unit of instruction, the teacher must make learning progressions clear. This clarity includes student-friendly rubrics. A team's defined mastery for each standard and skill they expect to assess serves as the foundation for team-created rubrics and student self-assessment. If teachers on a team can agree on what mastery in a specific skill looks like, they can articulate to students the expectations and specify exactly what students need to know or do to achieve mastery. This is when they create those rubrics.

Consider the rubric in figure 3.8 (page 76) as a beginning point for articulating the progress a student will make as they learn a new skill. This is only a guide for what teachers will put into their rubrics; it is not specific to any skill, subject, or grade. Notice, at each progression level, there is a clear description of what the student will know and be able to do. Teachers use this as a guide when they create their own specific rubrics with their teams.

1—SUPPORTED	2—APPROACHING	3—MASTERED	4—BEYOND
The student demonstrates elements of approaching mastery but requires constant support to do so.	The student understands the vocabulary and can demonstrate some elements of mastery, but does so inconsistently.	The student regularly uses the vocabulary and consistently demonstrates mastery of the skill as determined by the team or teacher.	The student demonstrates mastery of the skill and is able to apply this at an advanced level or in a real-world situation.

Figure 3.8: Rubric with descriptions of each progression level.

In the example of the mastery rubric in figure 3.9, a coach helps the team clearly define each mastery level with student-friendly language.

Learning Target: I can develop and use a model to describe how gravity and inertia keep objects in orbit.			
1—SUPPORTED	**2—APPROACHING**	**3—MASTERED**	**4—BEYOND**
With assistance, I can *recognize forces* that exist that cause objects to move.	I can define gravity and inertia, and I can *analyze a model* to identify the force of gravity and property of inertia.	I can *develop and use a model* to describe the role of gravity and inertia in orbital motions of objects in the solar system.	When provided with various scenarios, I can *analyze data* in the solar system to determine changes in gravity and inertia.

Source for standard: Nebraska State Board of Education, 2017.
Source: © 2022 by Teri Pay, Kengie Gass, & Amy Hunt. Used with permission.
Figure 3.9: Example secondary science rubric.

Through these rubrics, students should be able to understand and identify where they are with each step of the learning process and what they can do to improve their understanding of the skill.

Another way to make learning progressions clear to students is through the classroom setup. Showcasing the four critical questions of a PLC on the board and writing the answers to those questions for students provides the clarity students need in order to understand the skill being learned. Another option to include in your classroom is a standards and skills wall. It can look different for many different teachers and subjects, but essentially, the wall should include the standards and skills the students will learn throughout the school year, what they are currently learning, and evidence of skills already learned.

Coaching strategies for supporting teachers as they clarify learning progressions follow.

- **Ask teachers the following questions to ensure they can clarify learning progressions for students.**
  - → "What does a more in-depth knowledge of the skill look like?" (This relates to the students who need extensions.)
  - → "What does the skill look like for students who are close to defined mastery?" (These are the students approaching mastery.)
  - → "What are your students able to do with peer and teacher support?" (This relates to the students who need interventions.)

- **Encourage teachers to collaborate and share their experiences with learning progressions.** Create opportunities for them to engage in grade-level or subject-based teams where they can discuss what has worked for students. This can also be done through learning walks where teachers observe how their peers present these progressions to their students in an active classroom.

Step 2: Respond to Students' Learning Progress

Coach teachers to provide specific, actionable, timely feedback throughout a unit of instruction. That consistency is vital because, as Hattie has said, what teachers learn during it "helps [them] modify instruction, see the effects of their teaching so far, and hints as to where to go next in their teaching" (Hattie & Zierer, 2018, p. 19). Encourage teams to collaboratively select two or three formative feedback prompts from the following list to determine where students are with a particular skill.

- **DOK level 1: Recall and reproduction**
  - → On your white board, **list** the order of operations.
  - → **Label**, from memory, the parts of a plant.
  - → With a partner, use flashcards to **recall** your multiplication facts.
  - → Take five minutes to **memorize** the plot diagram. Then **match** the words to the correct line on the diagram.

- **DOK level 2: Using a skill or concept**
  - → With a partner, **summarize** _____ in twenty words or fewer.
  - → Work with your group to **categorize** _____ .
  - → After reading the first page, **predict** what will happen to _____ .
  - → **Distinguish** the differences between _____ and _____ .

- **DOK level 3: Strategic thinking or reasoning**

    → **Construct** an argument about _____ and support it with text evidence.

    → **Compare** your incorrect geometry problems with a partner to determine common errors.

    → Before completing the lab, **hypothesize** the outcome with at least one sentence of sound reasoning.

- **DOK level 4: Extended thinking or complex reasoning**

    → **Design** your own lab about _____.

    → **Critique** the sources used in the sample essay and **analyze** whether the sources are credible.

    → **Apply** percentages by **creating** a real-life way to use them while shopping.

The feedback prompts should be consistent across the team to create continuity from teacher to teacher. The team members determine what the correct responses to these prompts sound like.

The following strategies are for coaches supporting teachers as they learn to respond to students' learning progress.

- Regularly observe teachers' instruction and provide constructive support about the clarity of the teachers' own feedback. Encourage teachers to reflect on their responses and make adjustments as necessary.

- Help teachers analyze data based on feedback prompts. Help them identify patterns, strengths, and areas for improvement.

Step 3: Involve Self- and Peer Assessment

Student self-assessment is an effective way for students to reflect on their own learning and make specific choices and goals that further their education. This creates a sense of ownership. Just as teachers are expected to be students of their curricula and understand the why, students can be held to that belief as well.

For students to be able to self-assess honestly, they must understand that learning is a progression. Students can self-assess informally through conversing, or more formally through grading themselves on a team-created rubric, like the one in figure 3.10. Notice that some of the rubrics in this chapter have only three levels of understanding because level 1 represents students who need intense teacher support through the entire skill.

Another example of a self-assessment is in figure 3.11 (page 80). Notice that students are rating their level of understanding. They also have to show proof of where they are.

Directions: Use this rubric to decide whether you have reached mastery on the assignment. Read each item and assess your own mastery level. Check off the items you have mastered, and add a statement saying how you can improve that skill. Address all items in the Approaching Mastery column until you are at least at a 3—mastery level.

Where You Extended Expectations:	Criteria for the Assignment:	Where You Could Improve Your Work:
4—ABOVE MASTERY	**3—MASTERY**	**2—APPROACHING MASTERY**
Topic Sentence ☐ The topic sentence includes the title, author, and topic. ☐ The topic is accurate. **How can I apply this to the real world?**	**Topic Sentence** ▨ The topic sentence includes the title and author. ☑ The topic is basic. **What is my plan to reach above mastery?** Add more detail.	**Topic Sentence** ☑ The topic sentence is missing the title, author, or topic. ☑ The topic is inaccurate. **What is my plan to achieve mastery?**
Supporting Details and Theme ☐ Three big supporting details or events are given in the correct order. ☐ The overall big idea or theme is correct and thoughtful. **How can I apply this to the real world?**	**Supporting Details and Theme** ▨ Three big supporting details or events are given in a varied order or are basic. ▨ The overall big idea or theme is given. **What is my plan to reach above mastery?** Add more detail.	**Supporting Details and Theme** ☐ Big supporting details or events are missing or may be incorrect. ☑ The overall big idea or theme is not supported by the text. **What is my plan to achieve mastery?**
Organization and Grammar ▨ The punctuation is fully correct. ▨ Transitions are fully correct. ▨ The format of summary is correct through the use of a close-reading outline. **How can I apply this to the real world?**	**Organization and Grammar** ☐ The punctuation is mostly correct. ☐ Transitions are basic or mostly correct (3 out of 4). ☐ The format of summary is correct. **What is my plan to reach above mastery?**	**Organization and Grammar** ☐ The punctuation is incorrect and affects the meaning. ☐ Transitions are missing. ☐ The format of summary is incorrect. **What is my plan to achieve mastery?**

What mastery level did you initially give your summary, and why?
I gave myself a 3 because that is what I checked off.

Teacher-determined mastery level: 2
☒ Needs intervention

If intervention was needed, how did you improve your mastery level?
I made a better topic sentence and thought up a theme.

Figure 3.10: Student self-assessment, middle school example.

ESSENTIAL QUESTIONS:

- What is the discounted price of an item?
- How can you determine the original price of an item after a price increase or decrease?
- How do you find the sales tax on an item?
- What is the percent error or percent change of an event?
- How much should you leave for gratuity?
- What is the simple interest earned on a savings account or loan?

LEARNING TARGET:	YOUR PROOF:
I can find the percentage of a number.	**Your Proof:**

RATE YOUR LEVEL OF UNDERSTANDING:

1	2	(3)	4

Your Proof:		
15% of 70 =	$/70 = {}^{15}/_{100}$	10.5
9% of 18 =	$/18 = {}^{9}/_{100}$	1.62
36% of 60 =	$/60 = {}^{30}/_{100}$	18
3% of 26 =	$/26 = {}^{3}/_{100}$	0.78

SCORE ON THE QUIZ:

LEARNING TARGET:
I can use proportional relationships to find a percent increase (markup and tax). (7.RP.3)

RATE YOUR LEVEL OF UNDERSTANDING:

1	(2)	3	4

SCORE ON THE QUIZ:

Your Proof:

Your food bill at a restaurant is $24. The sales tax is 6%. What do you owe? You also decide to leave a 20% tip. What is the total cost of your meal now?

$24/ = {}^{26}/_{100}$

92.30

LEARNING TARGET:
I can use proportional relationships to find percent error and percent change. (7.RP.3)

RATE YOUR LEVEL OF UNDERSTANDING:

1	2	3	4

SCORE ON THE QUIZ:

Your Proof:	**Accelerated**
After finishing an experiment, John finds that the mass of a brick he weighed was actually 33.4 grams. Mr. Todd thought it was 32.7 grams. What was his percent error?	At a supermarket, a certain item has increased from $0.75 per pound to $0.81 per pound. What is the percent change in the cost of the item?

Figure 3.11: Student self-assessment, secondary mathematics example.

Using the rubrics as a guide, students evaluate themselves to better understand where they are in terms of mastery. The student who completed the self-assessment in figure 3.12 was originally at mastery. She chose to complete what she needed in order to show that she was above mastery after intervention.

4—ABOVE MASTERY	3—MASTERY	2—APPROACHING MASTERY
Topic Sentence and Concluding Sentence	**Topic Sentence and Concluding Sentence**	**Topic Sentence and Concluding Sentence**
☑ The topic sentence is thorough and clear. ☑ The topic sentence conveys the paragraph's main idea clearly. ☐ The concluding sentence is reworded.	☑ The topic sentence is clear. ☐ The topic sentence conveys the paragraph's main idea basically. ☑ The concluding sentence is restated.	☐ The topic sentence is developing. ☐ The topic sentence does not convey the paragraph's main idea. ☐ The concluding sentence does not refer back to the topic sentence.
Evidence of above mastery: *The topic sentence comes from the plot and the main idea.* ④	**How I can make it better:** *The topic sentence explains what happens in the article and shows the main idea. The concluding sentence is in fact restated.*	**How I can make it better:**
Evidence—Standard W.9	**Evidence—Standard W.9**	**Evidence—Standard W.9**
☑ There are three carefully evaluated, specific, and relevant cited facts. ☑ All three cited facts have correct, carefully chosen transitions. ☑ All three cited facts have fully correct in-text citations. ☑ Evidence drawn reflects a sophisticated understanding of the topic or task.	☑ There are three well-selected cited facts. ☐ All three cited facts have correct transitions. ☐ All three cited facts have mostly correct in-text citations. ☑ Evidence drawn reflects a clear understanding of the topic or task.	☐ One or two basic facts are cited, and they may not be specific. ☐ Transitions are missing. ☐ In-text citations are incorrect. ☐ Evidence drawn reflects a developing understanding of the topic or task.
Evidence of above mastery: *All three cited facts have matching transitions. All three cited facts have the correct citations.* ④	**How I can make it better:** *Cited facts were all carefully looked over.*	**How I can make it better:**

Figure 3.12: Student self-assessment, middle school English language arts example.

After this student turned in the rubric, her teacher reassessed the summary using the same rubric on the same piece of paper that the student used. The teacher indicated that the student needed intervention and, with the check marks, easily gave the student feedback on what needed improvement. After looking at the rubric and the teacher's feedback, the student was able to edit what she originally missed, and also articulate to her teacher what she missed.

Use the question bank in figure 3.13 to help teams determine actions they might need to take for high levels of learning to occur.

The following strategies are for coaches helping teachers provide student self-assessment.

- Help teachers analyze the data they get from using student-completed rubrics. They can look at what interventions worked best, how many students were able to move up a level, and what extensions students completed.

- Use the self-assessment as a way to look at very specific evidence teachers are using to determine mastery. This makes it easier for coaches to provide targeted feedback and to understand what mastery looks like for a specific skill.

- Ask questions to prompt teachers to clarify the need for student self-assessment.

- Have teachers take the student self-assessment to determine whether they are being clear enough for their students. A coach can also complete a rubric to gauge the clarity for students as well.

Is mastery clearly defined?	Are there opportunities for students to help their peers?
Is mastery defined on a student-friendly rubric?	Are the skills broken down into achievable parts?
Are students engaged?	Do the students interact with the rubric by checking boxes and making comments about progress?
Are students *compliant* and merely doing something to please the teacher?	Are there formative questions to help determine where students are in their learning progression?
Are students actively engaged in their own learning by assessing and articulating their progress?	Do students practice each skill and receive immediate feedback?
Are there processes in place for students to monitor their own progress?	What types of progress monitoring are being used?
Are there processes in place to give immediate feedback?	Are students given the opportunity to set and reach goals?
Are there opportunities for students to check and fix their own work?	Are students able to see how they grow from the beginning to the end of the unit?

Figure 3.13: Question bank—Student ownership and self-assessment.

Reflect to Elicit Change

After implementing new strategies to engage students in active learning, coaches can carefully guide teams through reflection and steps for improvement. Through conversation about team strengths and challenges, your goal of developing teams through transformational coaching may be realized, with them collectively reflecting on and adjusting their individual and collective practices. From this, a sense of confidence builds in both teachers and students. As you help teachers do this work and complete the first part of the team coaching inventory in figure 3.14, school becomes a place of learning and not simply point chasing for students.

	START	STOP	CONTINUE
ACTION THREE: STUDENT OWNERSHIP AND LEARNING PROGRESSIONS	Providing a graphic organizer to track learning and feedback for each writing skill on a rubric	Being the "giver" of grades	Providing clear rubrics for students
SMART Goal	For each skill on a graphic organizer, indicate whether a student achieved mastery in the specific skill, and provide feedback to each student once a week for the duration of each unit.		
Reflection	Initially we thought this would take a lot of time to implement—and it did, but it was worth it. We saved time on the back end because more students passed the CFA at the end of the unit. Our students stayed more engaged because they felt more confident in their learning. The feedback helped both the student and the teacher know what was needed and was focused on a specific skill.		

Figure 3.14: Example of team coaching inventory, action three.

Don't Miss This

Be aware of the following things while leading and coaching the journey.

- **The clearer the expectations are, the more manageable a teacher's and student's jobs are:** Having clear expectations for students also creates very clear expectations for a team's instruction. This would greatly help a teacher who may be new to a team.

- **Not every student will respond all the time:** The beauty of this system is that the majority of the class will be engaged in self-learning so the teacher can find and focus on struggling students *during* the unit of instruction—not after, when it is too late.

- **Read more about student self-assessment:** For additional ideas regarding student self-assessment, we recommend *You Can Learn! Building Student Ownership, Motivation, and Efficacy With the PLC at Work Process* by Tim Brown and William M. Ferriter (2021).

- **Rethink assessment as part of the *Simplifying the Journey* process:** This enables students to become much more engaged in their own learning and provides teachers with information regarding their learning and a teacher's practices. The resulting assessments (whether they are student self-assessments or a team's shared formative assessments), combined with targeted feedback, provide one of the most powerful tools in a teacher's tool belt. In the next chapter, we will explore ways for teachers and teams to utilize assessment results to increase learning and determine the effectiveness of their strategies.

Answering critical question two:

"How will we know when each student has

acquired the essential knowledge and skills?"

(DuFour et al., 2016, p. 36)

Utilizing Formative Assessment for Feedback

Formative assessment combined with specific, actionable feedback is ideally a frequent part of a teacher's and team's practice, and cohesive enough not to interfere with the natural flow of various elements within the teaching and learning process. Thoughtfully embedded assessment allows teachers to gather real-time feedback regarding where a student is in their learning journey and gain feedback regarding the impact of the instructional strategies.

Just as PLC members are taking part in a collaborative process, formative assessment itself is a process. It is a knowledge check to elicit information from a student about the current learning and the impact of a teacher's selected strategies. That means both students and teachers benefit from frequent formative assessments. This valuable insight allows the teacher to adjust or refine a selected strategy or practice throughout the unit to better support student learning. According to John Hattie (2015):

> The major purpose of assessment in schools should be to provide interpretative information to teachers and school leaders about their impact on students, so that these educators have the best information possible about what steps to take with instruction and how they need to change and adapt.

Because of feedback's importance, leaders and coaches can help teams understand the valuable information received from consistent use. As explained in table 4.1, formative assessment as a tool for learning provides three specific types of valuable feedback: (1) feedback for the teacher, (2) feedback for the student, and (3) feedback for instruction.

Table 4.1: Forms of Feedback

FEEDBACK FOR THE TEACHER	FEEDBACK FOR THE STUDENT	FEEDBACK FOR INSTRUCTION
The teacher receives information that helps them determine *where the learner currently is* on the path to mastery.	The teacher provides targeted, descriptive feedback to the student recognizing *areas of strength and next steps* on the path to mastery.	The teacher receives essential feedback from student responses regarding the *effectiveness of the current teaching strategies*.

The next action in *Simplifying the Journey* is for teams to commit to using formative assessment for feedback about student learning. Teams can be confident they are using formative assessment combined with feedback when the following become part of their instructional practices.

- They have clearly communicated what mastery of the learning targets being assessed looks like.

- They identify and share the specific strengths of students' learning toward mastery of the targets.

- They provide descriptive next steps for students as they progress toward mastery of the standard.

- They make instructional adjustments during the unit based on feedback.

Leading the Work— Specific Actions of School and Team Leaders

Leaders can take the following specific actions to clarify and communicate the work to be accomplished; support teachers as they learn together; monitor the work; and validate and celebrate teams as they learn to formulate and use formative feedback.

Clarify and Communicate the Work

Research shows that formative assessments are the checks that are most effective in student growth. W. James Popham (2013) writes, "Formative assessment works. That's right: ample research evidence is now at hand to indicate emphatically that when the formative-assessment process is used, students learn better—lots better."

In addition to conveying how crucial it is to conduct the assessments, it's important to communicate that formative assessment is not a test but a process used by collaborative teams throughout instruction to provide feedback for the educator and student as they learn. Because formative assessment is a valuable tool for monitoring learning and providing instructional strategy feedback, there is a valid rationale for why it may not be suitable to use as part of a student's grade.

- Formative assessment *focuses on the learning process* and a student's *progress* toward mastery of a standard or learning target.

- Formative assessment provides a space for students to *show their progress*, *learn from mistakes*, and *take risks* they might not otherwise take on an assessment that is linked to a grade.

- Formative assessment allows students and teachers to *embrace the process of learning* rather than the accumulation of points toward a grade.

These checks for understanding should occur frequently during the instructional unit and should be short enough to quickly evaluate where a student is on their path to proficiency. Feedback will be received and provided in three forms that the team and school leader can convey to teachers (as seen previously in table 4.1).

Support Teachers as They Learn Together

Visit classrooms frequently! Identify teachers and teams who are utilizing formative assessment and feedback effectively. Next, create opportunities for teachers to share *how* they are utilizing formative assessment and feedback as part of their instructional practices. You can accomplish this a variety of ways.

- Dedicated time during an already-established faculty meeting

- Dedicated faculty learning sessions

- Short videos of a teacher using formative assessment combined with feedback (Share these videos with staff through an email or a common online repository. You could also create a QR code that takes teachers to the videos and post it in the faculty lounge. QR Code Generator [www.qr-code-generator.com] and Canva [www.canva.com/qr-code-generator] are two examples of QR code generators.)

- Learning walks where teachers visit different classes and observe colleagues

As mentioned, giving teachers and teams opportunities to share their work is also a form of validation and celebration that models what the work looks like and reinforces teams' practices.

Monitor the Work

Visiting the classroom frequently and, before or after, asking for specific evidence is key to monitoring this action. As leaders engage in frequent, intentional classroom visits, the following questions provide valuable information regarding strengths they can celebrate and areas where they can assist their teachers.

- "How are you frequently assessing students throughout your lessons each day?"

- "Is the feedback you're providing descriptive and focused on the following things?"
  - → The strengths the student is demonstrating on their path to proficiency
  - → Targeted assistance and next steps for areas where the learner may be struggling

- "What have you learned about the strategies you are using from feedback you're receiving from your students?" (For example, if a teacher discovers that many students are providing incorrect answers in formative assessments, this powerful feedback means the teacher can then shift strategies or practices during the unit. Likewise, if a teacher discovers that most students have responded well to a formative assessment, this reinforces that the strategy the teacher chose is effective and important to share with other team members.)

- "What adjustments are you making to your instruction based on the feedback?"

Validate and Celebrate Teams as They Learn

It's important to remember that formative assessment for feedback is one of the most powerful tools a teacher can utilize in the classroom, yet it is often underutilized. As such, this will often be a change in practice for a teacher. As with learning any new skill or practice, feedback is key. Connecting the application of formative assessment to feedback in the classroom is essential.

Organizational experts Marcus Buckingham and Ashley Goodall (as cited in Siggins, 2020) explain that "what most people want is attention and they are more productive and engaged when regular, positive feedback is given." This feedback is critical to supporting a teacher's and a team's growth, but more importantly, it also validates the work the team is engaged in fulfilling.

When validating the work of teachers and teams, keep in mind a few tips for providing validating feedback (Siggins, 2020). They apply to students as well as to adults.

- **Provide frequent and timely positive feedback:** Validate the team's work as soon as the task or event occurs. Waiting too long may make the recipients feel their work has gone unnoticed.

- **Be genuine and specific:** Avoid using general validating comments. Instead, use specific examples from the teacher's or team's practice.

- **Understand your people:** Some people prefer recognition that's public, while others prefer private validation. Knowing your teachers and teams allows you to personalize feedback to each personal and team style.

Coaching the Work—
Specific Actions of Learning Coaches

Student ownership and self-assessment lead directly into teachers' use of formative assessment. You could argue that a teacher cannot have one without the other, in fact. Students' active involvement in their own learning decreases the amount of time a teacher spends grading and forming feedback about assignments and frees up time for them to spend with individual students and specific skills.

Consider This Scenario

> A fifth-grade team has designed a science unit about the earth's systems. The teacher team uses a series of skills that follow a process similar to the scientific method. They make it so that students experience how to (1) analyze and interpret data, (2) use mathematics and computation, (3) form questions and investigate, (4) develop a model to explain their investigations, and (5) design solutions to problems that occur. Students receive a topic and are told to have each step completed at the end of three weeks. Teachers supply a brief explanation of each step and allow students to work independently during science time each day for the duration of the unit. Some students work diligently, while others are often off task.
>
> At the end of the three weeks, teachers collect the projects and start the task of grading them and writing feedback on them. The teachers don't have time to intervene, and most students don't seem engaged or interested, so the grades remain the same and the feedback is ignored. Students disregard the feedback because they have too much to do right now keeping up in class; teachers feel the same way and move on also.

Strengths are as follows.

- Students know the required steps and receive instruction for each.

- Students have time to complete the assignment at school, where there are ample resources.

The scenario leaves the teachers and the students in a rough spot. Here are their challenges.

- The only time teachers gather evidence of learning is at the end of the unit, when the projects are turned in.

- The only time feedback is given is after the unit has ended and future units have already been taught and assessed.

- A process is provided to guide students, but the opportunity to internalize and learn is lacking because so much time passes between the learning and the feedback.

- The teachers in the scenario inadvertently reaffirm the myth that students who are learning at high levels can learn and students who are struggling to gain mastery cannot learn. Because the teachers do this, the students who are learning at lower levels lose hope in their abilities, and the teachers lose hope in their ability to impact students.

Coaching considerations for this team follow.

- **Encourage the team to find ways to quickly assess each step in the process:** Things to look for and plan for might be as follows.

  → What did the *teacher* learn about the students and their learning progression?

  → What did the *student* learn about their personal learning journey?

  → How is instruction going to change to meet the needs of the students?

- **Help the teachers and the team develop a plan to provide practice that includes a specific means for *immediate* feedback to increase student learning:** Students need to practice a skill before they are expected to complete it on their own. Try different strategies and maintain a growth mindset. Just like it is OK for students to need multiple chances, teachers might need that same grace and support as they embark on a new journey.

Plan and Gather Evidence

Providing teachers with the knowledge of what formative feedback through assessment looks like in a classroom is critical to feedback's success. The keys to successful formative assessment in a classroom follow.

- Stating expectations clearly
- Assessing a specific skill
- Evaluating assessments for validity
- Providing timely, actionable feedback
- Applying grade norming as a team for valid results

As a team prepares for its unit of instruction, a customizable "Targeted Unit Plan" reproducible (page 106) guides the team to use its previously established essential standards as they design instruction, prepare for shared formative assessments, and commit to actions for specific days throughout. Figure 4.1 and figure 4.2 (page 96) are elementary and secondary examples of the targeted unit plan. Note that the quantity of learning targets, vocabulary words, lessons, and so on, can change depending on the unit length and number of targets.

Unit of Instruction: Writing a paragraph

Beginning Date: August 23	Ending Date: September 10

CRITICAL QUESTION ONE: What knowledge, skills, and dispositions should every student acquire as a result of this unit, this course, or this grade level?

Essential Standards Addressed in This Unit:

I can write one well-developed paragraph.

Critical Academic Vocabulary:

Cited evidence, analysis, transitions, main idea, topic, and concluding sentence

Formative Feedback Prompts:

1. What facts would you select to support . . . ?
2. What information can you gather to support your idea about . . . ?

CRITICAL QUESTION TWO: How will we know when each student has acquired the essential knowledge and skills?

Target One and Mastery	Target Two and Mastery	Target Three and Mastery	Target Four and Mastery
The topic sentence conveys the main idea.	Cited facts are relevant with grade-level transitions.	Analysis sentences explain and add to the cited fact.	Writing is free of mechanical and spelling errors.
Target Five and Mastery	**Target Six and Mastery**	**Target Seven and Mastery**	**Target Eight and Mastery**

CRITICAL QUESTION THREE: How will we respond when some students do not learn?

During-Unit Intervention and Dates	Proven Strategies
Informational close reading outline common formative assessment intervention	This helps students closely read their articles with a purpose. They are able to use the graphic organizer effectively when writing a paragraph.
Cited fact common formative assessment intervention	Do students understand the reasoning behind a cited fact?

CRITICAL QUESTION FOUR: How will we extend the learning for students who are already proficient?

During-Unit Extension and Dates	Proven Strategies
Read higher grade-level articles.	Look at leveled articles and find one that is a grade or two higher than the grade being assessed.
Students choose their topics and articles.	Give the students five options to choose from.

continued →

Directions: Items listed here are agreed-on daily actions of a team's unit plan. As you plan your unit of instruction, agree on what action will occur each day during the unit. (There may be more than one action that takes place per day.)

Preassessment (one time) Instruction	Common formative assessment (two or more times) Data review (two or more times)	Intervention or extension (to be determined) End-of-unit assessment (one time)

DAY 1	DAY 2	DAY 3	DAY 4	DAY 5
Action:	**Action:**	**Action:**	**Action:**	**Action:**
Instruction	Instruction	Instruction	Common formative assessment; review data	Intervene/extend; review data
Resources:	**Resources:**	**Resources:**	**Resources:**	**Resources:**
Introduction to close reading outline	Close reading outline on own	Close reading outline on own	Close reading outline assessment	Informational close reading outline extension and intervention
Notes:	**Notes:**	**Notes:**	**Notes:**	**Notes:**

DAY 6	DAY 7	DAY 8	DAY 9	DAY 10
Action:	**Action:**	**Action:**	**Action:**	**Action:**
Instruction	Instruction	Common formative assessment	Intervene or extend	Instruction Intervention or extension
Resources:	**Resources:**	**Resources:**	**Resources:**	**Resources:**
Introduce cited facts	Cited fact practice with magazine	Cited fact common formative assessment	Cited fact extension and intervention	Introduce analysis sentences

Notes:	Notes:	Notes:	Notes:	Notes:

DAY 11	**DAY 12**	**DAY 13**	**DAY 14**	**DAY 15**
Action:	**Action:**	**Action:**	**Action:**	**Action:**
Instruction	Instruction	Unit assessment, review data	Intervene or extend, review data	n/a
Resources:	**Resources:**	**Resources:**	**Resources:**	**Resources:**
Introduce topic and concluding sentences	Well-developed paragraph as a class high/low example	Well-developed paragraph assessment with self-assessment	Well-developed paragraph assessment, extension, and extension or intervention	n/a
Notes:	**Notes:**	**Notes:**	**Notes:**	**Notes:**

END-OF-UNIT REFLECTION		
Start (what to begin doing)	**Stop (what didn't work)**	**Continue (what worked well)**
Look at the well-developed rubric with the new standards coming out next year.	Do we need more time to teach? With library lessons now taking more time away from in-class instruction, what do we need to drop? Do we need to extend?	Testing specific skills that led up to the skill of writing a paragraph.

Source for standard: Utah State Office of Education, 2013.

Figure 4.1: Targeted unit plan, elementary example.

UNIT OF INSTRUCTION: 7.2.4: The theory of plate tectonics

Beginning Date: October 24	**Ending Date:** November 16

CRITICAL QUESTION ONE: What knowledge, skills, and dispositions should every student acquire as a result of this unit, this course, or this grade level?

Essential Standards Addressed in This Unit:

1. A student is able to define the concept that the earth's crust is divided into plates that are moving above the earth's asthenosphere.
2. A student can explain the cause-and-effect relationship between convection current and plate movements.
3. A student is able to analyze data to understand that patterns exist in the physical features of the earth's crust, which leads to the theory of plate tectonics.

Critical Academic Vocabulary:

Asthenosphere, lithosphere, convection current, convergent boundary, divergent boundary, transform boundary, Pangaea, continental drift theory

Formative Feedback Prompts:

1. Describe the earth's lithosphere.
2. How does the heat from the earth's core create convection currents?
3. What evidence do scientists have for the theory of plate tectonics?

CRITICAL QUESTION TWO: How will we know when each student has acquired the essential knowledge and skills?

Target One and Mastery	Target Two and Mastery	Target Three and Mastery	Target Four and Mastery
A student can describe that the earth's lithosphere is divided into plates that move due to convection currents.	A student can diagram the earth's asthenosphere, with convection current motion, to provide evidence for plate movement.	A student, when given evidence pieces, can argue that the plates of the earth's crust are moving.	A student can explain patterns that exist (mountain ranges, rift valleys, earthquakes, and so on) that provide evidence for plate boundaries.
Target Five and Mastery	**Target Six and Mastery**	**Target Seven and Mastery**	**Target Eight and Mastery**

CRITICAL QUESTION THREE: How will we respond when some students do not learn?	
During-Unit Intervention and Dates	**Proven Strategies**
Convection currents, November 4	Mrs. Mansell used lava lamps within the intervention. Students diagrammed convection currents within a lava lamp before making the connection to convection currents. After the lesson and reassessment, most students achieved mastery in this skill.
Evidence for plate tectonics, November 11	Mrs. Jones modeled the activity for students and chunked evidence cards for student groups. After a jigsaw of the chunked evidence cards, students completed a scaffolded formative assessment. Some students achieved mastery in this skill after a reteach and reassessment, but others needed an additional one-on-one intervention to be successful.

CRITICAL QUESTION FOUR: How will we extend the learning for students who are already proficient?	
During-Unit Extension and Dates	**Proven Strategies**
Convection currents, November 4	Students worked in groups of four to complete an escape room based on knowledge learned within the unit as well as puzzles for future curriculum within the unit.
Evidence for plate tectonics, November 11	Students viewed a Scrat short from *Ice Age: Continental Drift*. Using their knowledge of the theory of plate tectonics and the theory of continental drift or Pangaea, students identified "wrong science" in the cartoon and explained the real science that should have happened.

continued →

Directions: Items listed here are agreed-on daily actions of a team's unit plan. As you plan your unit of instruction, agree on what action will occur each day during the unit. (There may be more than one action that takes place per day.)

Preassessment (one time) Instruction	Common formative assessment (two or more times) Data review (two or more times)	Intervention or extension (to be determined) End-of-unit assessment (one time)

DAY 1	DAY 2	DAY 3	DAY 4	DAY 5
Action:	**Action:**	**Action:**	**Action:**	**Action:**
Preassessment Instruction	Instruction	Instruction	Formative assessment Data review	Intervention or extension
Resources:	**Resources:**	**Resources:**	**Resources:**	**Resources:**
Worksheet, colored pencils, slideshows	Candle, dish, water, food coloring, timer, worksheet	Candle, dish, water, food coloring, timer, worksheet	n/a	Intervention lab
Notes:	**Notes:**	**Notes:**	**Notes:**	**Notes:**
Student knowledge from sixth grade is assessed concerning convection currents. After a brief preassessment, students diagram the earth and include convection currents within the mantle.	A lava lamp is introduced as a phenomenon to connect with a real-world example of the idea of convection currents within the mantle. Students begin a lab.	Students complete the convection current lab.	Students take a quiz on convection currents. Students complete a lab analysis if needed.	Intervention or extension for convection currents

DAY 6	DAY 7	DAY 8	DAY 9	DAY 10
Action:	**Action:**	**Action:**	**Action:**	**Action:**
Instruction	Instruction	Instruction	Instruction	Intervention or extension
Resources:	**Resources:**	**Resources:**	**Resources:**	**Resources:**
n/a	n/a	n/a	n/a	n/a

Notes:	Notes:	Notes:	Notes:	Notes:
Students complete an activity of fact-or-fiction statements about convection currents and layers of the earth.	Students complete a Pangaea activity.	Students finish the Pangaea activity.	Additional evidence for the theory of plate tectonics is introduced.	All students are extended with additional current technology evidence for the theory of plate tectonics.

DAY 11	DAY 12	DAY 13	DAY 14	DAY 15
Action:	**Action:**	**Action:**	**Action:**	**Action:**
Formative assessment	Instruction	Instruction Data review	Instruction	Intervention or extension
Resources:	**Resources:**	**Resources:**	**Resources:**	**Resources:**
n/a	n/a	n/a	n/a	n/a
Notes:	**Notes:**	**Notes:**	**Notes:**	**Notes:**
Students complete a formative assessment using evidence cards. After discussing each evidence piece with their peers, students individually complete the assessment.	Students learn about plate boundary types through a lab using cookies.	Students analyze data from the lab and incorporate this information into their model of the earth and convection currents.	Students review for their unit assessment next week on day 17.	Students receive intervention or extension on the theory of plate tectonics.

END-OF-UNIT REFLECTION		
Start (what to begin doing)	Stop (what didn't work)	Continue (what worked well)
		Incorporating lava lamps when teaching phenomenon

Source for standard: Nebraska State Board of Education, 2017.
Source: © 2023 by Kristin Mansell. Used with permission.

Figure 4.2: Targeted unit plan, secondary example.

Next, coaches guide teachers in learning to use assessments as feedback. The following are specific ways for coaches to educate teachers on this topic.

- Create an environment where teachers use feedback to gain more knowledge (just as they do with students).

- Model effective feedback practices when you coach teachers.

- Provide training sessions where teachers can practice with each other.

- Use video recordings as examples of providing feedback.

- Share success stories and highlight different teachers in the school who have effectively used assessment as feedback.

Coaches must provide the following steps and resources for teachers to create effective assessments and feedback tools.

1. Clearly state expectations.

2. Assess a specific skill.

3. Evaluate assessments for validity.

4. Give timely, actionable feedback.

5. Perform grade norming as a team for valid results.

STEP 1: CLEARLY STATE EXPECTATIONS

A rubric not only clarifies how a teacher will assess but also lets students know exactly what they need to do to achieve mastery (as discussed in chapter 3, page 63). The metaphor that says it's impossible to hit a moving target applies here. Students cannot know or accomplish what they need for mastery without clarity. Teachers work to have that shared clarity with each other; coach teams to consider students part of the team in that aspect. The approach can look different for different people, but the general idea is that a teacher has made the rubric accessible, meaning it is on a student's paper or computer and in student-friendly language. The rubric's textual expectations of the skill also need to be clear. For example, *I can provide a piece of evidence from the text* is unclear, but *I can provide one piece of cited evidence from the article to support the main idea* is clear. Last, a teacher should review the rubric with students before assessing.

STEP 2: ASSESS A SPECIFIC SKILL

When teachers give large summative assessments, it is very difficult for them to drill down to how a student understands (or did not understand) a specific skill. If an assessment is determining a student's mastery in many skills, to disaggregate the information would be difficult and timely for the teachers. Using the skills mentioned previously (arriving at shared clarity and defined mastery, page 35), teachers must be able to pinpoint a single specific skill that a student needs to know for an assessment; this is vital for teachers in using assessments as feedback. A teacher can have a summative assessment for learning, but formative assessments along the way ensure that the teacher checks for understanding.

For example, in English language arts, one unit could be on writing one well-developed paragraph. Writing a paragraph includes quite a few different skills; however, within the unit, those skills will each be tested and broken down into a formative assessment. Consider the following.

- **Week one:** Informational close-reading formative assessment

- **Week two:** Cited-evidence formative assessment

- **Week three:** Analysis formative assessment

- **Week four:** Well-developed paragraph summative assessment

Assessments in weeks one through three target a very specific skill that students must know in order to write a quality paragraph. These provide students practice and allow teachers checks for understanding throughout the unit rather than one check at the end of the unit in a high-stakes summative assessment.

STEP 3: EVALUATE ASSESSMENTS FOR VALIDITY

When creating assessments, teachers must focus on their validity. While assessments won't always reveal the necessary data or be perfectly accessible to students the first time you give them, teachers should think about what they are testing and if it checks for student information they want. Teams may feel they need to adjust their assessments each year. Coaches can help them with that. In particular, make sure that teams can simply adjust assessments and do not have to reinvent the wheel each year.

To begin, help the team members keep the following in mind as they curate skill assessments.

- No more than ten questions appear on the assessment
  (and it's OK if it's only one question and it's not written down).

- All questions relate to that specific skill.

- A student can complete the test in one full period (or less).

- A clearly stated rubric is visible and comprehensible.

In addition to meeting those criteria, the team might need coaching as they confirm the following (or learn that the current assessments do not meet these criteria and need modifying or even scrapping altogether). Remind the team that it is OK to rework assessments for the following year. When teams create common assessments, the assessments will be as good as the teams' experiences. Creating rigorous assessments involves reflection afterward to determine their validity.

- Does daily classroom practice match the formative assessment's rigor? (For example, are questions on the assessment as difficult as those that students are being asked in the classroom on a regular basis? This would mean that teachers are providing questions of the same DOK level in class and on assessments. A coach works with teams by looking at data. Roughly 80 percent of the students should be passing an assessment. If *far fewer* than 80 percent are showing mastery, the classroom rigor might not be high enough to match what is being asked of students on the assessment. On the other hand, if *all* the students are passing the assessment, the coach can help the teachers make their assessments more rigorous.

- Does the formative assessment match the rigor of the summative assessment?

- Do all the assessments meet the rigor of the high-stakes test at midyear or the end of the year?

Webb's (1997) Depth of Knowledge is a reliable way to help teams determine rigor. Table 4.2 lists verbs, by DOK level, that benefit teams as they rework the rigor of assignments and assessments. The list of potential formative feedback prompts (page 77) has DOK-specific questions aimed at students, but it can be helpful for teams when they work on this.

Take these steps when using the following table.

1. Provide every team member a copy of table 4.2 prior to creating assessments.

2. Focusing on one skill the team wants to assess, discuss what verbs would be most effective.

3. Guide the team through creating questions that align with the verbs they want to use for the skill. Remember, they can form one question or ten, so long as the questions are *targeted*.

Table 4.2: Verbs for Determining Instructional and Assessment Rigor

RECALL AND REPRODUCTION VERBS			
Arrange	Find	Memorize	Respond
Calculate	Identify	Name	Restate
Define	Illustrate	Quote	State
Demonstrate	Interpret	Recall	Tabulate
Describe	Label	Recite	Tell
Develop	List	Recognize	Translate
Draw	Match	Repeat	Use
Explain	Measure	Report	

WORKING WITH SKILLS AND CONCEPTS VERBS			
Calculate	Demonstrate	Illustrate	Predict
Categorize	Determine cause and effect	Infer	Relate
Classify		Interpret	Separate
Collect and display	Distinguish	Make observations	Show
Compare	Estimate	Modify	Solve
Compile	Graph	Organize	Summarize
Complete	Identify patterns	Paraphrase	Use context clues
Construct			
STRATEGIC THINKING VERBS			
Analyze	Compare	Differentiate	Investigate
Apprise	Connect	Draw conclusions	Judge
Argue	Construct	Evaluate	Justify
Assess	Critique	Examine	Predict
Calculate	Debate	Explain phenomena in terms and concepts	Revise
Cite evidence	Decide		Use concepts to solve nonroutine problems
Classify	Develop a logical argument	Formulate	
		Hypothesize	
EXTENDED STRATEGIC THINKING VERBS			
Analyze	Create	Formulate	Propose
Apply concepts	Critique	Modify	Prove
Connect	Design	Plan	Synthesize

Source: Adapted from Glass, 2020.

*Visit **go.SolutionTree.com/PLCbooks** for a free reproducible version of this table.*

STEP 4: GIVE TIMELY, ACTIONABLE FEEDBACK

Assessment feedback can build hope in students. The concept of learning as a progression is something students can carry into all kinds of work and processes throughout life. Understanding that someone can see what you're doing and let you know how to improve is the reason for that hope. The idea that an assessment is a single data point to give feedback about where a student is in relation to mastery is more worthy of an educator's time and support. Simply put, an assessment of either kind is about feedback to both the student and the teacher in regard to the student's understanding of or ability with a specific skill.

The feedback from teachers to students looks different for every teacher and classroom. However, here are some suggestions for when coaching teachers on how to give feedback (and for when coaches give teachers feedback).

- **Timely:** Students remember what they did on their assessment. Feedback should take no longer than a week post-assessment. Not only is it important to give feedback throughout a unit, research proves it is important to provide that feedback as soon after an assessment as possible (Woolf, 2020).

- **Actionable:** Specifics linked to the essential standard or skill, with some teacher professional judgment, guide students' thinking (Coe, Rauch, Kime, & Singleton, 2020). These specifics build students' hope as they begin to realize they can do the assessment after the feedback.

STEP 5: PERFORM GRADE NORMING AS A TEAM FOR VALID RESULTS

Through gaining shared clarity about their standards, a team agrees on what mastery looks like for their students (as discussed in chapter 1, page 13). Inevitably, however, teams make mistakes and might find that what they want to assess may be different for each team member. Because of these differences, their rubrics or assessment foci may vary across classrooms.

One of the best ways to mitigate this is to grade-norm as a team prior to grading the assessments. Ensure teams have this on their agendas. To grade-norm, all teachers on the team get the same assessment done by the same student or students. The team members then individually grade the assessment on their own. During team time, the team members all bring their graded assessments and work through the rubric, understanding why the team graded that assessment or skill a particular way. This establishes what is called *inter-rater reliability*, and creates a validated, equitable way of determining student mastery across the team. This also helps clarify any misconceptions about the assessment—for instance, regarding the rigor level, the actual skill being assessed, or what the questions ask students to do and how that aligns with the learning target.

Reflect to Elicit Change

Coaching occurs as teachers reflect on the data gathered about student-to-teacher interactions, student-to-assessment interactions, student-to-student interactions, and teacher-to-assessment interactions. Changing actions slowly, and effectively, changes the systems within the school to focus on learning and student outcomes more fully, rather than teachers and their strategies.

As a team, decide on next steps. What is a specific action that needs to start to move the team forward? What is a specific action that needs to be left behind because it might stop the team and students from high levels of learning? What is an action that should be celebrated and used? Finally, set a goal, no matter how small or large, that will keep the team on the road to success. With that goal in mind, is there any support that will be needed, and from whom will the team get it?

Figure 4.3 is an example of action four in the team coaching inventory.

	START	STOP	CONTINUE
ACTION FOUR: FORMATIVE ASSESSMENT FOR FEEDBACK	Using targeted assessments throughout the unit that cover one skill at a time	Waiting until the end of the unit to provide feedback	Breaking the unit into smaller parts
SMART Goal	Provide a weekly common formative assessment to assess a specific skill within the unit of study, which will provide data for immediate feedback to improve student learning.		
Reflection	It took a mind shift to make quick, short assessments that cover one or two skills instead of longer assessments that include many standards and skills. In the end, it made turnaround time and feedback very manageable. This kept the students engaged and focused on current learning. We can still improve by being more specific and focused.		

Figure 4.3: Example of team coaching inventory, action four.

Don't Miss This

Be aware of the following things while leading and coaching the journey.

- **Encourage a growth mindset:** Be the teacher who uses challenging assessments to foster a growth mindset in students.

- **Higher standards are combined with support:** Understand that teachers are showing more tutelage if they hold students to a high standard while also supporting them and believing in those students.

- **Communicate expectations:** Clearly explain what mastery of the assessed learning targets will look like and provide descriptive exemplars of mastery work.

- **Note strengths and provide what to do next:** When providing feedback to students, identify and share specific strengths of the students' learning and descriptive next steps as they progress toward mastery of the standard.

- **Refer to and act on data:** Use formative assessment feedback to make instructional adjustments during the unit of instruction.

Targeted Unit Plan

Unit of Instruction:	
Beginning Date:	Ending Date:

CRITICAL QUESTION ONE: What knowledge, skills, and dispositions should every student acquire as a result of this unit, this course, or this grade level?

Essential Standards Addressed in This Unit:

Critical Academic Vocabulary:

Formative Feedback Prompts:

1.
2.
3.
4.
5.

CRITICAL QUESTION TWO: How will we know when each student has acquired the essential knowledge and skills?

Target One and Mastery	Target Two and Mastery	Target Three and Mastery	Target Four and Mastery

Target Five and Mastery	Target Six and Mastery	Target Seven and Mastery	Target Eight and Mastery

CRITICAL QUESTION THREE: How will we respond when some students do not learn?	
During-Unit Intervention and Dates	**Proven Strategies**

CRITICAL QUESTION FOUR: How will we extend the learning for students who are already proficient?	
During-Unit Extension and Dates	Proven Strategies

As you plan your unit, with your team, agree on actions that you will take every day during the unit. More than one action may take place per day. Besides the days, items shaded gray are agreed-on daily actions for a team's unit plan.

Preassessment *(one time)* Instruction	Common formative assessment *(two or more times)* Data review *(two or more times)*	Intervention or extension *(to be determined)* End-of-unit assessment *(one time)*

DAY 1	DAY 2	DAY 3	DAY 4	DAY 5
Action:	Action:	Action:	Action:	Action:
Action:	Action:	Action:	Action:	Action:
Resources:	Resources:	Resources:	Resources:	Resources:
Notes:	Notes:	Notes:	Notes:	Notes:

DAY 6	DAY 7	DAY 8	DAY 9	DAY 10
Action:	Action:	Action:	Action:	Action:
Action:	Action:	Action:	Action:	Action:
Resources:	Resources:	Resources:	Resources:	Resources:
Notes:	Notes:	Notes:	Notes:	Notes:

DAY 11	DAY 12	DAY 13	DAY 14	DAY 15
Action:	Action:	Action:	Action:	Action:
Action:	Action:	Action:	Action:	Action:
Resources:	Resources:	Resources:	Resources:	Resources:
Notes:	Notes:	Notes:	Notes:	Notes:

END-OF-UNIT REFLECTION		
Start (what to begin doing)	Stop (what didn't work)	Continue (what worked well)

Source: Adapted from © 2022 by Kim Monkres, 2022. Adapted with permission.

Answering critical questions two, three, and four:

"How will we know when each student has

acquired the essential knowledge and skills?",

"How will we respond when some students do

not learn?", and "How will we extend the learning

for students who are already proficient?"

(DuFour et al., 2016, p. 36)

Learning From Formative Data

Has this every happened to you? One year, you use a particular strategy to teach a concept and students learn like crazy! Afterward, you walk down the hallway a little taller, resisting the overwhelming urge to take a victory lap while exclaiming, "I'm unbelievably amazing!" The following year, with the *same concept* and the *same strategy*, students just cannot get to mastery. Why would this happen? The teacher is, actually, still unbelievably amazing. The strategy that the teacher landed with the previous students just does not have the desired effect with this particular group of students. A chosen strategy's impact on student learning is what teams should explore. When someone on a team identifies effective strategies, they share these powerful strategies with the other members.

Team formative assessment data are the information collected and analyzed by a collaborative team to do three things: (1) assess student progress toward mastery of standards and targets, (2) identify students who require extra time and support, and (3) identify and share those practices that are proving effective. To be clear, collaborative teams can identify essential standards, administer frequent team formative assessments, and even build in extra time and support for those students who require it, but if they are not using their team formative assessment data to learn together and increase their instructional effectiveness, they will never function as a true learning community of professionals.

When teachers review their shared data, it's critical for them to study a strategy's effectiveness for learning and not compare teacher to teacher. Failure to separate the teacher from the practice will most assuredly turn a shared data meeting into an emotional, often defensive discussion with the possibility of creating animosity within the team.

Consider the following scenario to better explain the pitfalls of failing to separate the teacher from the instructional strategy.

> Each Thursday, the three teachers on a second-grade team meet for their weekly collaboration meeting. In previous meetings, the team identified essential content-area standards, came to shared clarity and defined mastery for each essential standard, and most recently designed a short team formative assessment and administered it to students during the week. The focus for this day's collaboration is reviewing the data from their shared assessment and making instructional decisions based on them. As the team members begin, they learn that two of the three teachers' data reveal many proficient students. One comments, "I can't believe how well my students did!" Her comment is followed by an approving nod and a comment from the other teacher whose students show mastery: "Your kids did amazing! I'm thrilled that my students' scores were similar to yours."
>
> As these two team members celebrate their students' success, an uncomfortable awkwardness creeps in. The third team member reviews the disappointing results for her class. They are significantly below the results of the other team members. The team leader searches for a reason to justify the low scores and ease the teacher's embarrassment: "You just have some students who are more difficult than the other two do."

In this scenario, it's obvious that teachers quickly began comparing scores. Instead, the team leader in this scenario could have encouraged the team to identify the strategies or practices and then, using their shared data, identify those that seemed to resonate with the students.

This team scenario plays out in various iterations in collaborative teams across many schools. Well-intentioned collaborative teams utilize team formative assessments, and in reviewing their data, they begin to compare scores with each other, attaching the performance of their students to the teacher. Consistently reviewing team data is an essential part of the collaborative process—but comparing scores only stirs emotions, creates contention, and in the end does not benefit the team's learning nor the students'.

It's important to remember that as teams review their common formative assessment data, they must be clear on what the purpose is: to study the impact of their chosen instructional strategy on student learning. Leaders can help them accomplish this by asking specific questions of their data, separating the teacher from the practice, and of course encouraging the teachers to learn together.

Leading the Work—
Specific Actions of School and Team Leaders

Leaders can take the following specific actions to clarify and communicate the work to be accomplished; support teachers as they learn together; monitor the work; and validate and celebrate teams as they learn how to use formative data.

Clarify and Communicate the Work

For the team and school leader, the expectation that collaborative teams will review assessment data is crucial. By making it clear that you as a leader expect teams to use team formative assessment data to learn together, you can cultivate a culture of learning that encourages professional dialogue and sharing of best practices. As leaders encourage this as a foundational part of a team's collaborative efforts, teams will strengthen their collective instructional efforts and ultimately increase student learning.

Keep in mind that a natural default for teachers when reviewing data is to compare scores with one another (Baldwin & Mussweiler, 2018). As teachers share their students' data with their team and leader, they are often at their most vulnerable. No teacher wants to look inferior to their peers, and if their scores don't measure up, it's a natural response to defend oneself. When—or before—this happens, leaders reclarify the work of reviewing team assessment data: "We're here to learn together." It's important to teach and reemphasize this.

This distinction between teacher and instruction and results is critical! Rather than comparing each teacher's scores, teams instead identify the strategy that the teacher used and examine the impact the strategy had on student learning. For example, a team may meet during their collaboration time and discuss the essential standards and learning targets that are part of an upcoming unit, have a shared understanding of what mastery looks like, and identify which strategies each teacher will use during their instruction. Much like an action research project, teams can then use their team formative assessment data to study the effects of each strategy. As teams approach data in this manner, the conversations will turn from "Look at how well my students did on this assessment" to a much more productive "Let's see how students responded to the strategy each teacher used."

One of the most valuable yet underutilized questions a team or school leader can consistently ask is simply, "What did you learn from this?" As teams review their data, refrain from using judgmental statements about individual scores. Seemingly innocuous comments such as, "Wow, your students did great!" unconsciously send the unintended message, "I'm judging you based on your students' performances." Instead, cultivate a culture of learning by replacing unintentionally judgmental comments about teacher data with "What did you learn from this?" or "Which instructional strategy had the biggest impact on student learning?" Learning together is the essence of a true PLC and an essential for team growth.

Support Teachers as They Learn Together

There is a tremendous amount of shared adult learning that occurs as teams review the results of in-unit team formative assessments, but "improved student learning only occurs to the degree that teacher teams collaboratively analyze the results of each formative assessment using a predetermined protocol to assess the learning of each student, skill by skill" (Eaker, 2020, p. 191). We acknowledge an abundance of useful protocols are available for teams to analyze student data. For the sake of simplifying, we encourage teams to use a simple four-question protocol as they review their team formative assessment data and learn together.

You can simplify the process of learning together from data by guiding teams to ask the four questions of their data that are shown in figure 5.1.

Data Question One	Data Question Two	Data Question Three	Data Question Four
MASTERY	**EXTRA TIME AND SUPPORT**	**TEACHING STRATEGIES**	**QUESTION ANALYSIS**
According to our team's agreed-on definition of mastery, which students have mastered the skill or standard?	According to our team's agreed-on definition of mastery, which students need extra time and support?	Which teaching practices or strategies proved most effective?	Are there individual questions or skills that *our* students tend to struggle with?

Figure 5.1: Four data questions for teams.

*Visit **go.SolutionTree.com/PLCbooks** for a free reproducible version of this figure.*

Notice that these questions focus explicitly on agreeing on mastery, which was addressed in chapter 2 (page 35); identifying students who require extra time and support, which is addressed in chapter 6 (page 129); and examining the impact of the individual teaching strategies each team member used.

Monitor the Work

Monitoring the work of the team members as they review their common formative assessment data comes down to simply asking questions of the team that they asked of their data. As a reminder, reviewing and sharing data as a team creates vulnerability with teachers, so emphasize the idea that you're all learning together.

You can ask teams the following questions as they review their data.

- "Which students achieved mastery?"

- "Which students require extra time and support?"

- "What is your team's plan for students who require extra time and support?"
- "Which instructional strategies did the students respond to best?"
- "Have you shared these instructional strategies with your teammates?"
- "Are there specific skills that all students tend to struggle with?"

As leaders ask these questions of teams, they establish two very important learning foundations.

1. A culture of learning together, which is fundamental to developing collective efficacy

2. Targeted questions that serve as a blueprint for the team's expected work

Validate and Celebrate Teams as They Learn

As teams shift their focus away from the highly emotional practice of comparing scores with one another and begin to focus their efforts on learning together from the data, leaders can then begin to validate the *learning* and not necessarily the score. Comments from teams such as, "We discovered that students really learned from this graphic organizer," are proof that teams are engaged in effective data conversations. Recognize and celebrate that by acknowledging the teams are doing work that leads to professional growth and increased student learning.

Along with this, when teams share that students didn't respond well to a particular strategy, you need to validate that too; this is *team learning* from formative data. The confidence gained from asking targeted questions of their data, free of judgment, provides a simple pathway for teams to follow as they develop a culture of learning together.

Coaching the Work— Specific Actions of Learning Coaches

The previous chapter focused on coaching teachers and teams to use data as feedback to inform teachers, students, and instruction. This section details how to use data to determine who learned a skill and can move to deeper learning, who still needs support through additional time and intervention, and which strategies elicited the highest levels of learning. With these parsed data, teachers and teams can customize learning and truly get down to specific students and specific skills.

Consider This Scenario

A middle school mathematics team is meeting to reflect on their data from the team's recent formative assessment. All the members of the team have brought the student results for their respective classes. Five percent of

continued →

Teacher A's students didn't meet the determined level of mastery. Nearly one-third of Teacher B's class didn't meet the determined level of mastery. And 12 percent of Teacher C's students didn't meet the determined level of mastery. When the teachers meet to review the data, they quickly share their results with each other, briefly discuss the behavior of a few students, and finish by calendaring a few upcoming events occurring in the school.

At the conclusion of the meeting, the team members know that they must provide time to reteach the students who didn't demonstrate mastery, but they are unclear on exactly how. They quickly decide each teacher will take time to reteach their own students utilizing the same strategy used during the initial instruction, possibly slowing the pace. Along with this, Teachers B and C can't help but feel there must be a reason that their students' mastery levels weren't as high as Teacher A's. Thoughts like, "Teacher A has more capable kids than we do" and "I have more students who are IEP-entitled in my class," have begun creeping into their conversations.

It is obvious that this team is anxious to do the right work, giving a coach a number of strengths on which to build. The following are all reasons to validate the team members and celebrate with them.

- They work as a team and use collaborative formative assessments.

- They determine which students achieved mastery and which require additional assistance.

- They plan for some rudimentary extra time and support for those who require it.

Their challenges look like the following.

- **Lacking a clear protocol for reviewing data:** Members of the team become emotional and begin to rationalize reasons for their students' underperformance. Due to their lack of understanding of how to learn from their data, the team members choose to provide extra time and support for their own students and utilize similar strategies to those used during the initial instruction.

- **Not using the team's collective strengths:** The number-one indicator of success is collective teacher efficacy—the belief that together, we can make a difference (Hattie, as cited in Waack, 2018). We can impact learning. How do teachers and teams achieve this mindset and bring it to fruition? They share strategies that seem to have led to learning; send students to the teacher whose students showed high levels of learning for intervention; and work collaboratively to design meaningful extensions for all students.

Coaching considerations for this team follow.

- **Help them think differently:** Their review of their assessment results appears to be a superficial analysis of the data. Instead of focusing on the percentage, they can focus on a specific student and the specific skill that needs intervention. By doing so, they will make their intervention much more than a review where every student participates in the same learning. Instead, the learning will target and support specific deficits. This will make their intervention efforts much more targeted with a greater chance at success.

- **Help them gather data:** Data collection requires much more than noting who passed and who didn't. Assessment questions should correspond to a specific skill. Teachers and teams should know the skill being addressed, not just a percentage of student mastery rates. Coaches can help teams create a way to gather data and use the data collection features of their learning management system. They can coach them to provide more, smaller, skill-specific assessments.

- **Help them work collectively:** Foster conversations that focus on student learning, not teacher success or failure. Change the language to revolve around how students learn, instead of thoughts such as, "You were great" and "I was horrible." When the focus turns to how students responded, instead of a teacher's alleged success or failure, team members become much more willing to share and learn from each other.

Plan and Gather Evidence

Once a team has answered the four data questions for teams in figure 5.1 (page 118), the team will benefit from focusing their conversations on the data prompts in figure 5.2.

TARGETING ASSESSMENT
What is the skill being assessed? Did we assess the target correctly?
Look at the very targeted assessments and the skill that is being assessed. Because the assessments should be so specific, the teacher should be able to pinpoint exactly what the student is missing. This makes interventions and extensions so much easier to assign and more valuable.
EMPLOYING DATA-FOCUSED TEAM TIME
Who did not perform the skill or target?
Consider using a shared form (document or excel) with teachers specifying by name which students did not understand the skill.
Consider using a shared form (a document or spreadsheet) with teachers and specifying by name which students did not understand the skill.

continued →

Why did they not perform? Was it because of a certain situation, a lack of true understanding, attendance, or something else?

While meeting as a team, discuss the reasons for students' not learning the skill. Was there a holiday, so many students were gone? Was the teacher gone for a few days, so maybe the students did not learn as much? Does a student struggle with reading and there was a long passage? Did a student have a rough morning and have a behaviorally difficult time? Because there could be many different reasons as to why students did not learn, teachers should talk with their teams about students they are especially concerned about and patterns to students or classes and respond accordingly.

Who performed beyond the skill or target?

Identifying the students who performed beyond the skill will help in two very important ways. First, it will provide an opportunity for the teacher and team to determine whether the assessment met the rigor needed to master the standard. Second, it will provide information for the team to identify students who need to be challenged for deeper learning in the essential standard or skill.

What do they need to know now to deepen their understanding?

Determining what a student can do to deepen their understanding is sometimes difficult for a teacher. The following list describes some ways to determine this.

- Look at the next grade-level essential standard and how it deepens for them.
- Have students connect that skill to a real-life example.
- Have them teach it to another student.
- Have those students explain in their own words why or how they were able to learn that skill.

UNDERSTANDING BEST PRACTICE FOR THAT TARGET OR SKILL

Which instructional strategy or activity was most effective for students?

- What strategy elicited the best learning results?
- Did different strategies elicit high results? How could these varying strategies work for various students?
- Did any strategies specifically help special needs students?
- How can the team take the best practices and apply them to the next unit or lesson?

Have an open and honest conversation about which teaching strategies or activities had the biggest impact on student learning. Many teachers tend to feel that data are very personal reflections on themselves as teachers. This shouldn't be the case. Instead, when looking at data, teams need to study the impact of the instructional strategy. In doing so, the team studies instructional strategies and not individual teachers. Only then can a teacher team eliminate the emotion from data meetings and focus on which instructional strategies significantly impacted student learning.

Figure 5.2: Data prompts for teams.

*Visit **go.SolutionTree.com/PLCbooks** for a free reproducible version of this figure.*

As teachers and teams consider different ways to learn from their formative assessment data, teams may benefit from coaching on different types of data. It is time to gather some evidence around student work. Coaching can require helping teams look beyond pass/fail rates and decipher the reasons behind those numbers. Start by separating student work into piles that indicate if the work is supported, foundational, mastered, or advanced. Figure 5.3 has descriptors your team can use.

1—SUPPORTED	2—FOUNDATIONAL	3—MASTERED	4—ADVANCED
Learning Descriptor:	**Learning Descriptor:**	**Learning Descriptor:**	**Learning Descriptor:**
The student is able to demonstrate elements of a 2 and 3 but requires constant support to do so.	The student understands the vocabulary and can demonstrate some elements of a 3 but does so inconsistently.	The student consistently demonstrates mastery as determined by the team or teacher.	The student demonstrates mastery and is able to apply this at a deeper level or in a real-world situation.

Figure 5.3: Student work descriptors.

Most teams will stop there, but that is not quite far enough. Guide the teams as they work together to describe that actual work.

1. **Post the following questions during the team data meeting.** When the team can answer the following questions, they are on their way to finding the skill that requires addressing.

   → *"What did the students do?"* Describe the work of students in each mastery level; also, describe the strengths and weaknesses of student work at each level. Determine if the work is a good indicator of mastery regarding the learning targets. Did instruction hit the mark?

   → *"What patterns do you see?"* Refer to learning targets and proficiency rubrics. Is there a pattern of misunderstanding to address? Are specific students repeatedly showing up as needing intervention? Which strategies seem to produce the best results?

   → *"What misconceptions become apparent?"* Based on those patterns, is there a specific skill to reevaluate or reteach? Do teachers have shared clarity— in other words, are they all on the same page?

2. **When determining how to proceed with the compiled student data, ask the team to differentiate between *instruction deficits* and *student deficits.*** A discussion about separating themselves from their students' scores is helpful. Focusing the discussion on strategies instead of perceived teacher success or failure is very important. Lead a discussion about when learning was impacted. Is it a whole-class issue, or is it an issue for a small portion of the class? Maybe it goes even deeper than that and the teacher needs to refresh with students some prerequisite skills. Use the data to shed light on how to respond using each of the following RTI tiers.

   → **Tier 1:** This is grade-level classroom instruction, and all students receive it. In the team scenario (page 119), Teacher A's students responded well to the instruction. It's wise to delve deeper into the specific teaching practice and activities that teacher used. Did those practices impact high-level learners? Did they impact those students who struggle? Are they considered best practices that all learners can benefit from? What strategies have worked in the past? Why was the strategy in Teacher A's class successful, and how did it differ from the strategy used in Teacher B's class? Teacher B in the scenario might need to look at the Tier 1 practices and fix some misunderstandings in the classroom before deciding about Tier 2 help.

→ **Tier 2:** In this tier, students who need extra time and support to keep up with grade-level work get adaptations and interventions. By delving into the specific needs of students, team members can tailor intervention to specific student needs and skills instead of broad strokes that only consider pass/fail. Warn the team not to believe the "misconception that adapting tasks waters down the curriculum and does not allow academic challenge" (Zapata & Brooks, 2017, p. 49).

→ **Tier 3:** Students whose learning has gaps that are beyond their grade level work with interventions, supports, and modifications at this RTI level. Team members can evaluate why a student's performance requires this need by examining patterns in wrong answers in the content area. Patterns across content areas are also beneficial. Consulting special education teachers, caregivers, and other teachers can add insight to any mental or physical disability that might be present. Some students, described as *twice exceptional*, "have giftedness and a disability" and might need to be discussed also (Zapata & Brooks, 2017, p. 8). It is just as important to recognize the student who is bright and struggling.

3. **Pose the following questions.**

→ *"What elements should we incorporate to obtain enough data to really get down to the student or skill level?"* Discuss practice assignments with the team. Does the practice assignment help students learn new skills? Does it align with a specific target? Are the rigor of the practice and the rigor of the assessment the same? Also discuss how the assessment has been formatted. Can teachers easily distinguish which questions align with which skills? Are the assessments short and targeted to allow for immediate feedback? This discussion is very helpful *before* a unit or lesson has been given, but reflecting after the fact is also helpful to refine teaching practices.

→ *"What needs to be discontinued?"* Time is a constant issue for teachers. Therefore, using data to streamline lessons is helpful. Coaches can lead and participate in a team discussion about the strategies and activities that have a direct impact on learning. Do the questions assess a specific skill? Is the rigor too light, just right, or too difficult for the grade level? Also, can students complete the assessment in a reasonable amount of time? Can it be shortened to cover only the necessary material?

→ *"How can team members assist each other to ensure that all students are receiving the same high-quality education?"* Teachers are required to be part of the PLC process. Collective teacher efficacy demands that teachers come together. Therefore, relying on others to be successful is important. Merely acknowledge which strategies were helpful and try to incorporate them across the team. Sharing students is a highly effective way to do this. Some schools have a designated intervention and extension time built into their schedule.

→ *"Have team members aligned rigor from instruction to the formative assessments?"* Sometimes students perform really well on the practice assignments but then do poorly on the formative assessments, and vice versa. Coaches and teams can look at the instruction and assessment DOK levels to ascertain if they are the same. Look at assignments and assessments side by side to ensure they align.

Once teams have answered these questions and listed students and the skills they need extra help with, teachers and teams need to make a plan of action. Chapter 6 provides an in-depth process to help with the creation of extra time and support at the Tier 2 level. The Tier 3 level will be different at every school. It is important to know the additional support that is available to teams at your school. Ask your administrator. If no support is available, collaborate to formulate a plan of action that will work for you and your team.

Use the question bank in figure 5.4 to determine which strategies the team needs in order to use data to inform instruction.

Do teams and teachers use data from multiple sources such as the following? → Daily practice → Informal and formal common formative assessments → Summative assessments → End-of-level district testing results, state or provincial testing results, or other high-stakes testing results	Are common errors identified?
	Are those errors specifically addressed?
	Have teachers differentiated between instruction deficits and student deficits?
Do the results of daily practice, common formative assessments, summative assessments, and end-of-level testing align?	Have effective practices been identified?
Do teams analyze student work?	Are teachers learning from each other through collegial discussion?

continued →

Is student work broken into these mastery levels?	What additional knowledge checks can be incorporated to increase student learning?
→ Supported → Approaching → Mastered → Extended	Is the rigor the same from instruction to common formative assessment?

Figure 5.4: Question bank—Learning from formative data.

Reflect to Elicit Change

After processing the aforementioned material, what did the team learn? Did the instruction elicit the desired outcome? Can you or an administrator supply any additional resources or training?

As teams get better at these practices year after year, student learning will increase. As teams see success from these practices, they become agents of change. Agents of change can then impact the entire culture of a school, district, and educational system. Create the next action by completing the team coaching inventory, an example of which is in figure 5.5.

		START	STOP	CONTINUE
ACTION FIVE: LEARNING FROM FORMATIVE DATA		Looking at student performance during instruction	Focusing on percentages as our gauge of success	Meeting on a regular basis to talk about data
SMART Goal		When we are discussing data, we will describe the characteristics of the supported, foundational, mastered, and advanced levels of student work in order to determine the specific skills that are deficient.		
Reflection		Instead of focusing on pass/fail, we focused on skills because we listed what students were actually doing. We were able to provide meaningful feedback and provide immediate help to students. We also know what needs to be fixed next time around because we know some of the mistakes students are making and can integrate it into our daily lessons.		

Figure 5.5: Example of team coaching inventory, action five.

Don't Miss This

Be aware of the following things while leading and coaching the journey.

- **Use data to pivot:** The focus of learning from formative data is for teachers and teams to collectively study and respond to student learning and the impact of their instructional strategies on learners.

- **Ask important questions of your data:** As teams study their formative assessment data, they ask four questions of their data.

    → Which students achieved mastery?

    → Which students require extra time and support?

    → Which teaching practices elicited the best results?

    → Are there individual assessment questions students tend to struggle with?

- **This is about learning together, not comparing scores:** Team learning is critical to fostering student growth; as educators collectively improve their instructional practices, students learn more.

- **Read more about formative assessment:** For additional information regarding common formative assessments, we highly recommend *Common Formative Assessment: A Toolkit for Professional Learning Communities at Work, Second Edition* by Kim Bailey and Chris Jakicic (2023).

What if, during the instructional unit and following your in-unit assessment efforts, your team discovers that they still have a few students who have not yet achieved mastery? How do leaders and coaches help teams respond during the unit of instruction when students don't learn? The final step in *Simplifying the Journey* details how to provide extra time and support for students within the team.

Answering critical questions three and four:

"How will we respond when some students do

not learn?" and "How will we extend the learning

for students who are already proficient?"

(DuFour et al., 2016, p. 36)

Creating Extra Time and Support for Learning

Despite everyone's best planning and efforts, some students will not grasp a concept in a given unit. It's a function of humanity! If we know that humans learn at different rates and in different ways, and we can accurately predict some students will need extra time and support, members of a PLC can plan for and design ways for students to receive targeted help to learn during the unit of instruction and after the unit is completed. How do we provide extra time and support for the student who requires it? This is a perplexing dilemma to be sure, but it is solvable. Likewise, when a student takes little time to master an essential standard, educators are faced with a challenging dilemma.

This chapter focuses on helping teachers and teams create extra time and support in the classroom for students who require it to master a standard, and students who already have reached mastery and can deepen their learning.

Leading the Work— Specific Actions of School and Team Leaders

Leaders can take the following specific actions to clarify and communicate the work to be accomplished; support teachers as they learn together; monitor the work; and validate and celebrate teams as they increase their instructional effectiveness.

Clarify and Communicate the Work

Often, teachers hesitate to add a day (or more) to a unit because there is urgency to *cover all the standards*. Leaders continue making a compelling case for prioritizing each course's standards, identifying those that the teacher and team will work to ensure all students know and are able to do. Reiterate that when teams prioritize and identify essentials, this is the focus of their team formative assessment and intervention efforts. Repurposing an instructional day to focus on extra time to ensure learning of the essentials will shift a team's focus away from covering everything and more toward ensuring learning of the essentials. Consider the unit cycle of instruction in figure I.2 (page 5).

Building in a day (or days, depending on the unit's duration) during the unit for extra time and support for students who need it demonstrates a commitment to differentiation and serves as an acknowledgment by the team that some students need extra time. It essentially shifts a team's practices from a focus on teaching to a focus on learning.

Support Teachers as They Learn Together

Supporting teams as they move through their instructional cycles is critical to the teams' success. Keep in mind that as a leader, you are looking for evidence of the work. Be cautious of creating an abundance of forms or templates for teams to show their work. Instead, allow teams the autonomy to choose how they will show evidence that they can get to the student who has not yet achieved mastery and the skill they're not proficient in. Consider a fifth-grade team of teachers who are generally considered tech wizards, known for their prowess with anything technology related. They might produce a color-coded spreadsheet with the names of students who do not yet show mastery and the skills for which the students need extra support. Conversely, technology might not be a third-grade team's strong suit. They might use a binder to list the students who have not yet achieved mastery and the skills they are still working on.

Both teams show evidence that they are able to get to the student and the skill not yet mastered; they each accomplish it in a way that works for them. Providing each team the autonomy to show evidence of the work being expected lets the teams utilize their strengths, creates ownership, and in the end produces the evidence that you are expecting to see.

Monitor the Work

Frequently attend a team's collaboration meetings and ask for evidence of their work so you can identify strengths and specific areas where the team can benefit from coaching.

Ask questions with the intent to determine if the team is intervening at the learning target level and if extra time and support is required for mastery. Questions leaders may pose during a team meeting are as follows.

- "What are the names of the individual students who are not yet proficient in the essential standard or skill?"

- "How is your team providing extra time and support during the unit for those who need it?"

Validate and Celebrate Teams as They Learn

As teams produce evidence that they are identifying the specific students who have not yet achieved mastery *and* they are providing extra time and support during instruction and as a team, leaders need to recognize the shift that is occurring—a shift away from teaching standards to focusing as a team on ensuring students learn certain essential standards and skills. Validating teams and celebrating them are appreciable ways to recognize and show appreciation for their work and affirm their collective efforts. Don't miss the opportunity to validate and celebrate this shift in individual and collective practice! Consider the ideas listed in figure 6.1 to spur your discovery of creative ways to validate and celebrate the work of teams.

VALIDATING	CELEBRATING
Informal observations:	**Student success stories:**
Observe the team in action while they are intervening during the unit of instruction. Recognize students who are engaged and students who are making progress toward mastery of the standard or learning target.	Identify students who have made gains in learning because of the team's efforts. Share these stories with the team and school during informal conversations and in meetings.
Feedback from students:	**Social media:**
Gather informal feedback from students regarding their experience in receiving extra time and support, and share the feedback with the team.	Celebrate the work of teams with the school community through social media posts that include success stories, quotes from team members or students, and team photos.
Exit data:	**Faculty room visuals:**
Encourage teams to give short exit assessments. Compare the number of students who demonstrate mastery at the conclusion of the intervention.	Use the faculty room as a platform to celebrate the work of teams. Showcasing evidence of a team's work and the progress students are making with a comment section next to each allows fellow staff members to see the work and provide comments to the team.

Figure 6.1: Validation and celebration ideas.

Coaching the Work—
Specific Actions of Learning Coaches

Creating extra time and support is the last step in the process. It is a multifaceted process that includes both intervention and extension that helps answer the final two critical questions: "How will we respond when some students do not learn?" and "How will we extend the learning for students who are already proficient?" (DuFour et al., 2016, p. 36). For interventions, gathering sufficient evidence to narrow the focus to the exact student and skill is essential. For extensions, providing opportunities for students to continue to learn keeps students engaged in the learning process.

Consider This Scenario

An elementary science team gives an end-of-unit exam about moon cycles on Tuesday. On Wednesday, the team members bring the exams to a team meeting, where they quickly put their data on a spreadsheet with two columns—who passed and who did not. Twenty-three of Teacher A's students reached mastery, and seven did not. Twenty-seven of Teacher B's students reached mastery, and three did not. Thirteen of Teacher C's students reached mastery, and seventeen did not.

According to the data, Teacher B has had the most success. In turn, he shares his instructional strategy with his teammates, and they all reteach their individual classes. Students who have already achieved mastery have their skills reinforced, and those who have not yet achieved mastery get the opportunity to learn and show they learned the second time. Then, the intervention and extension are complete, and the team moves on to the next unit of instruction.

Strengths for this team follow.

- The team members created a spreadsheet to collect data and shared it among the team. They understand the need to collaborate and look at data to determine next steps.

- They list students by name in an attempt to understand individual needs.

- They share an effective strategy and use that strategy to increase student learning as a team, not as individual teachers.

Challenges in the preceding scenario look like this.

- The scenario team uses broad-stroke reteaching of the entire unit as opposed to targeted interventions with specific students and their specific deficiencies.

- Students who have achieved mastery are lumped with the rest of the group to reinforce skills, not truly extending those skills. They are not offered the opportunity to continue their learning.

Coaching considerations for this team follow.

- **Celebrate:** Take note of the actions that are moving a team in the right direction; a discussion about what is going well is appropriate. Then ask the hard questions to help the team course-correct. Those questions can focus on the scenario team's challenges, as they are typical of most teams. Regarding interventions, asking the following questions can guide teams.

  → "What specific skills are you assessing? Which of those skills need intervention based on the data?"

  → "If the team cannot determine those skills, what needs to change about the formative assessment to be able to compile those data?"

- **Pay attention to students who have achieved mastery:** If Tier 1 instruction goes well, around 80 percent of students will be ready for extended learning. It is important to have meaningful activities for those students. It is just as important for them to have a next step as it is for struggling students.

Plan and Gather Evidence

To best support students, engage teams in conversations about data, including identifying which students need what kind of support and when teachers (or others) can provide that support.

STEP 1: DISAGGREGATE THE DATA

Disaggregating specific data from an individual classroom can help team members identify the students who need extra time and support in the essential standard or skill. The reproducible "Extra Time and Support Data Collection—Individual Teacher" (page 142) is one way to do that disaggregation and examination. This tool is for an individual teacher's —or singleton's—use when looking at classroom data and chosen practices. Figure 6.2 (page 134) is an example of an individual teacher's data collection.

Notice the team has determined which intervention and extension strategies they are using. A team can do this before or during the unit depending on their experience with the content. In the example, the team has worked collectively for a few years and can say which intervention has worked specifically for this learning target. Having more than one type of intervention or extension is OK, because they may target different types of learners.

ASSESSMENT TITLE: RATIOS AND PROPORTIONS COMMON FORMATIVE ASSESSMENT	
Essential Standard and Skill:	I can decide whether two quantities are in a proportional relationship and describe what it means to be proportional.
Teacher:	Powers
Specific Intervention for This Assessment:	Support students to draw conclusions from the proportion to find the value of x.
Specific Extension for This Assessment:	Plan a grocery store trip that requires using unit rates and proportions to determine distance and cost.
Total Students:	147

In the following columns, list students by first name and last initial.

After the First Attempt: **RECEIVED A 1— SUPPORTED**	After the First Attempt: **RECEIVED A 2— FOUNDATIONAL**	**STUDENTS WHO WERE ABSENT**	After the Second Attempt: **FULLY SUPPORTED**
Students who demonstrate elements of levels 2 and 3 but require constant support to do so	*Students who understand the vocabulary and inconsistently demonstrate some elements of level 3*		*After intervention, students who need complete assistance (total attempts)*
Izzy R.	Chloe P.	Averlin A.	Russel K. (5)
Jaxson H.	Case B.	Toby S.	Drake D. (3)
Eliza M.	Sophie D.	Drake D.	Peyton C. (3)
Cayzlie G.	McKenna H.	Russel K.	
Oakley L.	Ellie M.	Easton O.	
	Ryker D.	Landon S.	
	Tavia G.	Max J.	
	Peyton W.		
	Shelby H.		
	Courtney C.		
	Isaac W.		
	Peyton C.		
	Reese W.		
	Swayde P.		
	Madison H.		
	Luke J.		
	Jillian S.		

Total students in this column:	Total students in this column:	Total students in this column:	Total students in this column:
5	17	7	3
Percentage of students who received a 1:	Percentage of students who received a 2:	Percentage of students who were absent:	Percentage of students who need full support:
(Divide the preceding number by the total number of students.)			
3%	12%	5%	2%

Figure 6.2: Example of extra time and support data collection—Individual teacher.

Notice that 15 percent of the students in this class were not showing mastery after the first attempt. Of that 15 percent, 3 percent needed constant support, while 12 percent could identify vocabulary and were close to demonstrating the skill.

This first attempt means that the initial assessment was given to students in class with everyone else. The students who are in the After the First Attempt columns did not pass that initial assessment but did pass after intervention. The assessments given to students for the second attempt can be the same or different depending on the team and test. The After the Second Attempt column is for students who are still not showing mastery after attempting the assessment a second time. These are students who need much more support than the students who passed after the second try.

Also note that after multiple attempts, three students still do not show mastery in the skill being assessed. Having three students who do not yet show mastery in a skill is OK. These are the students you pay closer attention to the next time you assess this skill.

STEP 2: DECIDE WHO WILL RETEACH AND WHO WILL EXTEND

How will the team you're coaching implement extra time and support for learning, whether it is intervening or extending?

- **Select a day:** Identify a dedicated day (or possibly more, depending on the length of the unit of instruction). No new instruction occurs on this day. Consider asking the following questions.
    - → "What is the team intervening on?"
    - → "Is it timely?"
    - → "Are you able to intervene (or extend) in that amount of time?"
- **Identify effective strategies:** Help identify and encourage the practitioners to share the instructional strategies that were most effective with the team. Consider asking the following questions.

→ "What practices elicited the best results?"

→ "With what particular students did different practices see results?"

→ "How are you going to extend for students?"

→ "Can you model the practice that was the most effective?"

- **Decide how you will intervene and extend:** Interventions can look like various approaches. Teams can extend a student's learning the following ways: "(1) go beyond the expected proficiency; (2) access . . . more of the required grade level curriculum; (3) access . . . above grade level curriculum" (DuFour et al., 2016, p. 170). Consider asking the following questions.

  → "What specific practice is the team going to use for intervention?"

  → "What extension model is the team going to use?"

  → "Who is going to teach the intervention and extension?"

  → "Are you planning to involve staff outside the team, such as aides?"

- **Share students:** Divide students among the team based on need, and allow them to spend the intervention and extension time receiving support with an identified proven strategy or with a teacher. "Sharing" students—working with students you don't have in the classroom—is vital for the success of all the students in the school. Sometimes students simply need a change of instructional scenery every once in a while. Sometimes students learn a skill via a different instructional strategy. Sometimes students benefit from working with peers who have gone beyond mastery. When teachers commit to this kind of collective responsibility and caring culture, they begin to realize the impact of collective teacher efficacy. Finally, consider asking the following questions.

  → "Did this particular intervention work? Why or why not?"

  → "Was this extension beneficial to students? Why or why not?"

  → "If (or when) you have to provide extra time and support again, is this the direction the team will go? Is there anything you would do differently?"

Before initiating a discussion about who will intervene and who will extend and how, talk deeply about extensions. Talk with the team about what "beyond" means to them. Is it the ability to teach the concept to someone else? Or maybe it's the ability to apply the concept to a real-world situation. Discovering what it means to the teachers who have contact with students every day is vital. Maybe the team wants to offer access to more in-depth curriculum. Consider the lesson plans that were put on the back burner earlier in the process as the team gave curricular priority to certain topics. For instance, the lessons that a teacher is passionate about but that were determined not to be critical or important—is there a place for them here? Finally, is there a need to extend students to the next level? Can you, in effect, start to front-load students with critical skills for the future? Is there a sense of curiosity instead of points chasing? What does it mean to extend learning?

Figure 6.3 (page 138), an example of the reproducible "Extra Time and Support Data Collection—Collaborative Team," (page 142) shows what a team would see when all members contribute to the document. What do you notice?

- Is the team able to articulate which group of students performed the best?

- Is the team able to identify how many students need intervention?

- Is the team able to identify how many students need constant support in intervention?

This team concludes that Teacher B will take the students who need intense intervention. Teacher A will take the students who need less intense intervention; this intervention could include simple changes or a quick reteach. Teacher C is slated to work with the students who need extended learning.

Inevitably, there are going to be roadblocks when trying to share students. No two teams, schools, or districts are alike, so coaches and teams need to get creative to implement this work. To best support teams, coaches need to be aware of two ideas that may hinder this work and address these concerns.

1. **Can interventions and extensions work in a singleton classroom?** Yes! Teams discuss and determine what practices worked best for students, but coach a singleton teacher to break their class into small groups around the room based on what the students need that day. Maybe the students who need intense intervention sit in the back one day with the teacher helping one-on-one. Maybe the students who need extensions sit in the front-left corner of the classroom because that's where they can access more of the supplies needed in their extension activity.

2. **Do interventions, extensions, and the sharing of students require a specific intervention time during the school day?** Not necessarily. These can be done at any time in the week or within the unit of instruction. Oftentimes, teams may come to realize during a unit that many of the students were absent the day they taught a specific skill. This could mean an adjustment in their schedule so that the extra time for support is during a specific class period or on a specific day.

ASSESSMENT TITLE: RATIOS AND PROPORTIONS COMMON FORMATIVE ASSESSMENT

Essential Standard and Skill:	I can decide whether two quantities are in a proportional relationship and describe what it means to be proportional.
Specific Intervention for This Assessment:	Support students to draw conclusions from the proportion to find the value of x.
Specific Extension for This Assessment:	Plan a grocery store trip that requires using unit rates and proportions to determine distance and cost.

Teacher: Brown   **Total Students:** 147

After the First Attempt: RECEIVED A 1—SUPPORTED	After the First Attempt: RECEIVED A 2—FOUNDATIONAL	STUDENTS WHO WERE ABSENT	After the Second Attempt: FULLY SUPPORTED (Total attempts)
Izzy R.	Chloe P.	Averlin A.	Russel K. (5)
Jaxson H.	Case B.	Toby S.	Drake D. (3)
Eliza M.	Sophie D.	Drake D.	Peyton C. (3)
Cayzlie G.	McKenna H.	Russel K.	
Oakley L.	Ellie M.	Easton O.	
	Ryker D.	Landon S.	
	Tavia G.	Max J.	
	Peyton W.		
	Shelby H.		
	Courtney C.		
	Isaac W.		
	Peyton C.		
	Reese W.		
	Swayde P.		
	Madison H.		
	Luke J.		
	Jillian S.		
Total students in this column: 5	**Total students in this column:** 17	**Total students in this column:** 7	**Total students in this column:** 3
Percentage of students who received a 1: 3%	**Percentage of students who received a 2:** 12%	**Percentage of students who were absent:** 5%	**Percentage of students who need full support:** 2%

Teacher: Turner   **Total Students:** 141

After the First Attempt: RECEIVED A 1—SUPPORTED	After the First Attempt: RECEIVED A 2—FOUNDATIONAL	STUDENTS WHO WERE ABSENT	After the Second Attempt: FULLY SUPPORTED (Total attempts)
Traygen W.	Kaylin S.	Conner B.	
	Max G.	Abigail B.	
	Sadie A.	Paul C.	
	Peter B.	Woods H.	
	Jacey W.	Alyssa Z.	
	Deshawn D.		
	Jax B.		
	Parker O.		
	Alex M.		
	Tyler H.		
	Damien H.		
	Jacob B.		
	Arlis M.		
	Easton M.		
Total students in this column: 1	**Total students in this column:** 14	**Total students in this column:** 5	**Total students in this column:** 0
Percentage of students who received a 1: 1%	**Percentage of students who received a 2:** 10%	**Percentage of students who were absent:** 4%	**Percentage of students who need full support:** 0%

Teacher: C			Total Students: 136	Teacher:			Total Students:
After the First Attempt: **RECEIVED A 1—SUPPORTED**	After the First Attempt: **RECEIVED A 2—FOUNDATIONAL**	**STUDENTS WHO WERE ABSENT**	After the Second Attempt: **FULLY SUPPORTED** (*Total attempts*)	After the First Attempt: **RECEIVED A 1—SUPPORTED**	After the First Attempt: **RECEIVED A 2—FOUNDATIONAL**	**STUDENTS WHO WERE ABSENT**	After the Second Attempt: **FULLY SUPPORTED** (*Total attempts*)
Carter M. Paige S. Adeline H. Carsen C. Skyler B. Dylan P.	Henry B. Ryder C. Jeff D. Jacob G. Alexis M. Degan S. Kaiden S. Charlee W. Tristan E.s Amberlyn H. Knox M. Matti S. Lanu T. Reese B. Brynlee B. Dakota B. Carter C. Remington H. Jesi M. Celton M. Molly W.	Briggs K. Stephanie L. Ana M. Manesh R. Simone F. Hodge F. Rilie T. Kamryn A. Rylan D. Tyler F. Wyatt J. Sariah L.	Lanu T. (3) Skyler B. (3) Kaden F. (5) Xavior M. (3)				
Total students in this column:	**Total students in this column:**	**Total students in this column:**	**Total students in this column:**	**Total students in this column:**	**Total students in this column:**	**Total students in this column:**	**Total students in this column:**
6	21	12	4				
Percentage who received a 1	**Percentage of students who received a 2:**	**Percentage of students who were absent:**	**Percentage of students who need full support:**	**Percentage of students who received a 1:**	**Percentage of students who received a 2:**	**Percentage of students who were absent:**	**Percentage of students who need full support:**
4%	15%	9%	3%				

What group of students best learned this skill?

Teacher B's students

What practices helped these students learn so much?

→ Very specific instructions

→ Slow release—whole-class work → group work → partner work → individual work

→ Memorable location activity (Teachers A and B used it as a practice.)

Figure 6.3: Example of extra time and support data collection—Collaborative team.

The question bank in figure 6.4 offers some questions to help start the conversation within a team about the next steps toward supportive interventions and powerful extensions.

FOR INTERVENTIONS:	FOR EXTENSIONS:
How can teams promote (among themselves and to students) the concept that it is OK if they still have not achieved mastery?	Can students go beyond the expected mastery on a skill?
Which strategies elicited the best results?	Can students access more than just those skills deemed essential by the team?
Is there a schoolwide time set aside for intervention and extension?	Can students access above-grade-level material?
According to the data, which teacher is best suited to teach an intervention?	What are some digital applications to help students go beyond?
Do teams have a plan to share students to reteach according to specific students and specific skills?	Are the extension activities student led?
How can the team's collective skills increase student learning?	Is there a choice menu figure 3.2 (page 69) for students to explore their own interests?
	Is the extension work independently completed by students, with the teacher acting as a facilitator?

Figure 6.4: Question bank—Extra time and support for interventions and extensions.

Reflect to Elicit Change

Now it's time to reflect. It is important at this point in the process to celebrate successes as well as ponder challenges. Celebrations for students and teachers are extremely important. Students need to see their growth, and teachers need to acknowledge their own success. For students, that might be the jump from completely supported work to some independent work. For teachers, it might be learning one new strategy that was very effective with certain learners (high or low) or seeing a once-struggling class succeed. Authentic reflection will reveal weaknesses, and those are not easy to face—but facing them allows you to help teams grow.

Determine the course of action by implementing a new action, letting go of the things that do not work, and celebrating the wins—and don't forget to ask for help. How can other teachers, coaches, and administrators assist the team on its journey?

Complete the team coaching inventory, an example of which is in figure 6.5.

	START	STOP	CONTINUE
ACTION SIX: EXTRA TIME AND SUPPORT	Looking at specific skills, not just percentages	Ignoring students who already get it	Looking at the results of our formative assessments
SMART Goal	After looking at the data, create immediate, meaningful interventions that focus on specific skills and specific students and at least one extension for each unit of study—divide and conquer using the collective skills of the team.		
Reflection	We worked on the interventions together after describing the student work, then shared our students based on need. This is an ongoing process that helps students feel confident in their abilities as they see success. The area we divided and conquered was extensions for students who already know it. We divided our units and each team member designed corresponding extensions. It was such a relief to have meaningful work for our students to deepen their learning. Our next step is to rotate the units and create additional extensions. The end goal is to have a choice menu created by numerous people to add variety for students.		

Figure 6.5: Example of team coaching inventory, action six.

Don't Miss This

Be aware of the following things while leading and coaching the journey.

- **Don't forget the students who already know it:** They are just as at risk of dropping out of school as students who struggle if they are not challenged during their educational journey.

- **Mind your culture:** Be cautious of creating a culture where interventions are viewed as punishments and extensions are viewed as rewards. Instead, the focus should be on creating extra learning time for all students.

- **Read some additional texts about the topics:** For additional ideas regarding creating schoolwide extra time and support for student learning, we recommend *Behavior Solutions: Teaching Academic and Social Skills Through RTI at Work* by John Hannigan, Jessica Djabrayan Hannigan, Mike Mattos, and Austin Buffum (2021) and *It's About Time: Planning Interventions and Extensions in Elementary School* and *It's About Time: Planning Interventions and Extensions in Secondary School* by Austin Buffum and Mike Mattos 2015; 2015).

Extra Time and Support Data Collection— Individual Teacher

ASSESSMENT TITLE:	
Essential Standard and Skill:	
Teacher:	
Specific Intervention for This Assessment:	
Specific Extension for This Assessment:	
Total Students:	

In the following columns, list students by first name and last initial.			
After the First Attempt: **RECEIVED A 1—SUPPORTED**	**After the First Attempt:** **RECEIVED A 2—FOUNDATIONAL**	**STUDENTS WHO WERE ABSENT**	**After the Second Attempt:** **FULLY SUPPORTED**
Students who demonstrate elements of levels 2 and 3 but require constant support to do so	*Students who understand the vocabulary and inconsistently demonstrate some elements of level 3*		*After intervention, students who need complete assistance (total attempts)*
Total students in this column:	**Total students in this column:**	**Total students in this column:**	**Total students in this column:**
Percentage of students who received a 1:	**Percentage of students who received a 2:**	**Percentage of students who were absent:**	**Percentage of students who need full support:**
(Divide the preceding number by the total number of students.)			

Extra Time and Support Data Collection—Collaborative Team

ASSESSMENT TITLE:						
Essential Standard and Skill:						
Specific Intervention for This Assessment:						
Specific Extension for This Assessment:						
Teacher:	**Total Students:**			**Teacher:**	**Total Students:**	
After the First Attempt: **RECEIVED A 1— SUPPORTED**	After the First Attempt: **RECEIVED A 2— FOUNDATIONAL**	After the Second Attempt: **FULLY SUPPORTED** (*Total attempts*)	**STUDENTS WHO WERE ABSENT**	After the First Attempt: **RECEIVED A 1— SUPPORTED**	After the First Attempt: **RECEIVED A 2— FOUNDATIONAL**	After the Second Attempt: **FULLY SUPPORTED** (*Total attempts*)	**STUDENTS WHO WERE ABSENT**
Total students in this column:	Total students in this column:	Total students in this column:	Total students in this column:	Total students in this column:	Total students in this column:	Total students in this column:
Percentage of students who received a 1:	Percentage of students who received a 2:	Percentage of students who need full support:	Percentage of students who were absent:	Percentage of students who received a 1:	Percentage of students who received a 2:	Percentage of students who need full support:	Percentage of students who were absent:

Simplifying the Journey © 2024 Solution Tree Press • SolutionTree.com

Visit **go.SolutionTree.com/PLCbooks** to download this free reproducible.

Teacher: _____ **Total Students:** _____

	After the First Attempt: RECEIVED A 1—SUPPORTED	After the First Attempt: RECEIVED A 2—FOUNDATIONAL	STUDENTS WHO WERE ABSENT	After the Second Attempt: FULLY SUPPORTED (Total attempts)
Total students in this column:				
Percentage who received a 1: / received a 2: / were absent: / need full support:				

Teacher: _____ **Total Students:** _____

	After the First Attempt: RECEIVED A 1—SUPPORTED	After the First Attempt: RECEIVED A 2—FOUNDATIONAL	STUDENTS WHO WERE ABSENT	After the Second Attempt: FULLY SUPPORTED (Total attempts)
Total students in this column:				
Percentage of students who received a 1: / received a 2: / were absent: / need full support:				

What group of students best learned this skill?

What practices helped these students learn so much?

page 2 of 2

7

Engaging in Focused, Productive Collaboration

It's virtually impossible to argue the critical nature of effective collaboration in a school. Whether it involves grade-level teams with shared content (such as a grade 11 English language arts team), vertical teams in the same curricular area (such as a middle school mathematics department), or virtual teams with shared content (such as a team of three band teachers from different high schools), purposeful collaboration is essential to increased team and student learning. When professional educators work in collaborative teams, sharing and learning together, their individual practices and collective efficacy increase because "when they return to their classrooms they will possess and utilize an expanded repertoire of skills, strategies, materials, assessments, and ideas in order to impact student achievement in a more positive way" (DuFour et al., 2016, p. 67).

Often, teachers have time to collaborate yet do not receive leadership or coaching guidance about what effective collaboration looks and sounds like. As a result, many collaborative efforts become loosely aligned department meetings that focus on various items that have little direct impact on student learning. The fact that teachers meet to collaborate will not significantly impact student learning nor their shared growth as a team. Instead, *what teams collaborate about* is what increases their effectiveness. As such, it's critical to clearly articulate expectations about a team's collective work and specific actions during their collaboration.

Leading the Work— Specific Actions of School and Team Leaders

Leaders can take the following specific actions to clarify and communicate the work to be accomplished; support teachers as they learn together; monitor the work; and validate and celebrate teams as they learn focused collaboration.

Clarify and Communicate the Work

Leaders may provide the time for teachers to collaborate and may even make a case for why it's fundamental to their work. Creating the necessary time for collaboration and clarifying why it's pivotal to learning are essential. Beyond that, leaders must also clearly articulate what effective collaboration looks like and how to effectively engage in it. Clearly established expectations decrease ambiguity and eliminate the question, "What are we supposed to do?"

Make clear to teams that creating team norms allows them to define specific actions and behaviors needed to maximize their time together. Communicate, as they begin creating (or revising) their norms, that norms that *do* work address specific behaviors. Table 7.1 has examples of norms that work and those that don't.

Table 7.1: Examples of Norms

BEHAVIOR TO ADDRESS	NORM THAT DOESN'T WORK	NORM THAT WORKS
Maximizing time together	Stay on task.	We commit to passionately focusing on the tasks we need to complete and remaining conscientious of conversational drift.
Addressing problems or challenges	Bring problems to the team.	We commit to spending time fixing problems rather than complaining by presenting two possible solutions for each problem shared.
Making decisions	Come to agreement.	When making decisions, we commit to hearing all voices and ensuring that the team's will becomes evident.

First, remind teams that one way to establish team goals and norms is to keep in mind the three big ideas that drive the work of a PLC (DuFour at al., 2016).

1. **A focus on learning**

2. **A collaborative culture and collective responsibility**

3. **A results orientation**

Then, as they follow the step-by-step process to create valuable, targeted norms, remind them how important they are to the work. It's important for teams to note the need to identify specific behaviors that prevent the team members from maximizing their valuable collaborative time. The following is a simplified process for the development of productive team norms (DuFour et al., 2016).

1. **Have each team member write on a sticky note a behavior that makes a collaborative meeting unproductive.** If the team needs anonymity, the team members can type up their ideas and print them out so their teammates do not see their handwriting.

2. **As a team, look for common themes among the behaviors and group these together, and turn each unproductive behavior into a productive statement.** Make sure the team begins each norm with *we commit* or *we will* to indicate commitment. For example, complaining about students, administration, or workload is an unproductive behavior. An effective norm addressing that behavior might be, *We commit to solve problems rather than complain by bringing two solutions for every problem presented to the team.* Is the team easily distracted, spending valuable time on anecdotal conversations? A norm could be, *We commit to stay ruthlessly focused and be conscientious of conversational drift.* Does someone talk the entire time? A norm might be, *We commit to hear and value all voices by utilizing an object that signifies the person who has it has the floor for no more than one minute.*

In terms of norms, teams decide on a way to ensure that everyone is following the norms. That might look like assigning a person who reviews the norms at the beginning of each meeting and then reminds the team when someone is violating a norm. Or teams might establish a visual cue to use for norm violation. For example, perhaps a team has a picture of a squirrel. If someone begins to violate a norm, any team member can pick up the squirrel picture as a reminder that, to maximize the team's valuable time, they need to adhere to their agreed-on norms.

Support Teachers as They Learn Together

As a leader creates time for teams to collaborate, provides clarity regarding what effective collaboration looks like, and uses strategic evidence-based questions to monitor the effectiveness of team collaborative efforts, it is important that the leader remember a few things regarding the development of collaborative teams.

- **Effective collaboration is a learned practice:** Just as teachers do not come to the profession fully knowing how to instruct on their subjects or how to manage a classroom, they won't necessarily come to the profession knowing how collaboration works to this end.

- **Teams will be at different places in their development:** Each team is unique. Don't assume that all teams in your school will progress at the same rate. Be patient and provide clarity and support as they learn together.

- **Teams won't require the same amount of time and support:** Some teams will be able to provide evidence for the work of each question that you ask, while others will struggle to provide evidence for the same questions. Use the collected evidence to decide how much time to allocate for monitoring and supporting the work of each team.

Along with providing teams with time, giving them resources to further their understanding of effective collaboration is critical. One such resource is the reproducible "What We Collaborate About" (page 160), which has questions that teams can ask of themselves while they collaborate. The questions guide teams through discussions as they plan for, learn from, and reflect on each unit. Those guiding questions align directly with the work that is introduced in each of the six actions in this journey shown in figure I.1 (page 4).

Monitor the Work

Monitoring collaboration may seem puzzling. It's not uncommon for leaders to attempt to monitor collaboration using one of the well-intentioned yet ineffective strategies listed here. Be cautious of these often-implemented—yet ineffective—strategies.

- **The go-forth-and-collaborate strategy:** In this misguided strategy, the leader provides time for teachers to collaborate yet rarely, if ever, visits or monitors the work of the collaborative team. The team is simply directed to "go forth and collaborate!"

- **The casual-observer strategy:** In this ineffective strategy, the leader will occasionally pop into a team's collaboration meetings and, from the doorway of the classroom, listen for a brief time, nod approvingly at the team's collaborative efforts, and vanish.

- **The front-row-seat-to-collaboration strategy:** Much like taking a front-row seat to a game or concert, the leader assumes a seat near the team and quietly observes the action taking place, occasionally adding validation or celebration (a high five or a "good job!") of the team's efforts.

- **The put-me-in-coach strategy:** In this misguided strategy, the leader is not content being on the sidelines and desperately wants to be part of the collaborative team. The leader jumps into the team's collaborative efforts by studying standards, reviewing data, and so on—essentially, doing the team's work.

Effectively monitoring focused collaboration means looking for evidence of the right collaborative work. Accomplish this by asking the questions in the reproducible "Monitoring Collaboration" (page 161).

Validate and Celebrate Teams as They Learn

A natural initial response for teachers and leaders is to find things that need correcting. Whether a student is learning a new skill, or a team is learning to collaborate, a leader might immediately look for unproductive thinking patterns or practices out of an inclination to help. Although it's important for helping move a team forward, shift the urge to correct from "What can I correct to help move this team forward?" to "Which steps in the process can I celebrate and validate with this team?" Recognizing and validating those steps that a team is doing well provides a positive foundation on which to build targeted support and next steps for the team. Utilizing the evidence-based questions in "What We Collaborate About" (page 160) and "Monitoring Collaboration" (page 161) allows the leader to identify those areas to celebrate and validate with the team.

Coaching the Work— Specific Actions of Learning Coaches

The preceding chapters have outlined six steps that help teachers become better practitioners and, in turn, increase student learning. *Collaboration* is the vehicle to accomplishing those steps, is the key to creating collective teacher efficacy (that sense that together, we can make a difference), and—within the same content areas and across the curriculum—is pivotal to the success of teams and students. Focused collaboration is how educators successfully implement the process outlined in this book.

Consider This Scenario

> A high school mathematics team informally meets in the hallway between classes, but rarely meets in a collaborative setting. After the school provides content teams a time to meet for common prep, the mathematics team members get together and schedule their time, but it seems like they're never on the same page, and disagreements occur regularly. Sometimes they don't even want to interact—so they don't. They understand the concept of using their collective skills but aren't sure how to get there. They rarely put their discussions into action. Just taking care of their own students is easier and makes the teachers feel more in control.

The team's strengths follow.

- The teachers are working hard.

- They are getting some results based on their data, but they just don't see the results directly correlating to their collaboration. They are unsure what the incentive is to meet when they need time to be successful in their own classes.

The team has a variety of issues to address.

- **Meaningful meeting time:** The team uses its built-in time to schedule but often skips it in favor of individual time.

- **Disagreements:** Team members can find common ground, but coaches can help them if they struggle.

- **Data:** Instead of listing who got something and who didn't, the team needs help making data meaningful.

- **Reliance on their collective skills:** The team, together, might instead ask if some students respond differently and why.

Coaching considerations for this team follow.

- **Focus on the right work:** The steps have been outlined, but the rest is not easy. Team members can fall into old practices because those are more comfortable. Explain why focused collaboration is important. The following section has some helpful processes and tools to make collaboration time meaningful, not just another meeting.

- **Remind team members that correctly collaborating about this process will eventually lead to more time for teachers to accomplish their tasks:** Famous author Stephen Covey (as cited in Brefi Group, 2014, p. 1) offers this advice: "create time to focus on important things *before* they become urgent." By intentionally following the process, the planning takes place and urgent matters become fewer, leaving more time for teachers because they don't have to spend as much time putting out fires.

Plan and Gather Evidence

Part of the necessary collaborative structure includes weekly collaboration meetings. Ask to go into team meetings. The reproducible "Weekly Team Meeting Agenda" (page 162) is one way to keep collaboration expectations top of mind. The example agenda in figure 7.1 focuses on the four critical questions. This form and format helps you gather information about how teams conduct meetings. Provide the template and let them answer these questions with a specific coach or as a team unit. Another way to gather the information is to watch a team meeting and note what you observe; then follow up with the entire team about what you learned. This could simply be a conversation about how the team members are collaborating at a high level and a time for the team to reflect. On the other hand, it could be a time for coaches to gauge the team's climate and how well they are collaborating. Provide the reproducible "What We Collaborate About" (page 160); it is teams' resource when trying to complete the questions on the agenda.

Time: 9:00–9:45 a.m.

OBJECTIVES

Look at the summary assessment data and discuss the best practices from this week when teaching an informational summary.

Determine interventions and extensions for tomorrow based on the data.

Look ahead at the next assessment, "Citing From Informational Text to Support the Main Idea." Grade the assessment as a team based on the rubric. Make any necessary changes.

Previous assessment: Summary assessment

DATA-FOCUSED ANSWERING OF CRITICAL QUESTION THREE: How will we respond when some students do not learn?	Best practices:
Based on assessment data, Teacher B will have the interventions.	Students determined the main idea from each paragraph and then worked on combining them into three big ideas. This seemed to help students condense a multipage article into only three big ideas. Color-coded or labeled ideas in each paragraph helped them organize the information.
DATA-FOCUSED ANSWERING OF CRITICAL QUESTION FOUR: How will we extend the learning for students who are already proficient?	Ideas for extensions:
Many of the students did quite well on this assessment, so we will have two classes of extensions.	Look at some real-world samples of texts that people have to summarize—legal documents, construction bids, and so on. Students can research what jobs require much summarizing.

INTERVENTION AND EXTENSION PLACEMENTS

Teacher A's focus:

Teacher B's focus:

Teacher C's focus:

Intervention:	Extension:
Students will be walked through the step-by-step process of writing a summary. The teacher will utilize color-coding to help students stay organized.	Students will look at real-world examples to create summaries.

Next assessment: "Citing From Informational Text" assessment

ANSWERING OF CRITICAL QUESTION ONE: What do we want all students to know and be able to do?	ANSWERING OF CRITICAL QUESTION TWO: How will we know if they learn it?
Students can cite from an informational text correctly. This should be in MLA in-text citation format.	We will be looking at the rubric for the assessment. Does it assess what we need it to assess? Teacher C will look on Purdue OWL (https://owl.purdue.edu) for any updates to the citation format.

continued →

ANSWERING OF CRITICAL QUESTION THREE: How will we respond when some students do not learn?	ANSWERING OF CRITICAL QUESTION FOUR: How will we extend the learning for students who are already proficient?
n/a	n/a
Next team meeting: September 20	

Figure 7.1: Weekly team meeting agenda example.

These weekly collaboration meetings should take no more than forty-five minutes. If the meeting is specific and targeted to the objectives, then the team can accomplish this. Are there going to be longer collaboration meetings? Sure! Many teams meet for a day or more in the summer to plan for the upcoming year. These meetings should still have norms and objectives and focus on the four critical questions. These meetings are also where this *Simplifying the Journey* process should begin.

While the agenda hits on all four critical questions, it is also flexible. Does the team only have enough time to talk about the previous assessment? Only use that section. Is the team's focus on the next assessment? Only use that section. The team members need not complete every section of the agenda. This is a team's weekly meeting, and they only have forty-five minutes. Do their objectives reflect forty-five minutes of work? Do the team members know what the team is focused on for the next few weeks? Are they collaborating and using various teachers' strengths?

At every weekly collaboration meeting, teams should focus on reiterating team norms, creating meeting objectives, using previous assessment prompts to guide team reflection, using upcoming assessment prompts to guide team discussion, planning how to address potential team roadblocks, celebrating team successes, and trying to head off conflict.

REITERATE TEAM NORMS

At the beginning of each meeting, teams should read aloud their norms as a reminder of their expectations and the commitments they've made to each other to maximize the use of their collaborative time. These are specific to the team. To read about creating norms, see page 148.

In terms of norms, which can reflect a team's cultural health (both what the norms are and whether members are following them), "Assessing Our Reality" (page 163) is for the team to thoughtfully complete a couple of times during the year. This tool is an attempt to cultivate the honest collaboration vital for teams to talk about and act on different aspects of their current reality. Ask them to reach out to you if they are struggling in one area or more.

CREATE MEETING OBJECTIVES

Having targeted, specific objectives for a team meeting is vital to the success of that specific meeting. These objectives will give the team guidance in what the team's discussion is about. These objectives can be as simple as, *Determine the next assessment,* or as complicated as, *Create a clear rubric for our assessment in two weeks.* The objectives must be attainable in the time allotted for the meeting. This ensures that conversation stays on task and has a specific purpose.

Be careful about putting too many objectives into a meeting. A forty-five-minute meeting should include no more than three objectives unless they can be completed quickly.

To determine what your meeting's objectives are, ask the team these questions.

- "What do we need to have completed by tomorrow?"
- "What do we need to have completed by next week?"
- "What do we need to have completed by the end of the month?"

For some meetings, you may just get through what you need to have completed by the next day. That is OK. Simply having objectives can continue keeping things on track.

USE PREVIOUS AND UPCOMING ASSESSMENT PROMPTS TO GUIDE REFLECTION

The data-focused conversations required here are detailed in chapter 6 (page 129), including prompts and considerations about what data reveal and how the team will address that.

PLAN HOW TO ADDRESS POTENTIAL TEAM ROADBLOCKS

What are some common roadblocks to teachers' work together? What do they look like? What should be the response to these challenges? See figure 7.2 for examples of roadblocks, what they might look like, and how a team can respond to those roadblocks.

WHAT THE ROADBLOCK LOOKS LIKE	WHAT THE TEAM'S RESPONSE SHOULD BE
ROADBLOCK: Seniority	
The teacher who has been teaching the longest has the final say on everything. They have been the team lead and department head for years with no one else being allowed a leadership role.	While the teacher who has taught the longest may have some great insight into teaching and best practices, new teachers also have some unique insights into what is current and updated in the teaching world. In order to build capacity in a school, leadership needs to be shared and rotated among the team. Each year, determine who will be the team lead and go on a rotation. This gives each teacher an equitable chance to be a leader and experience what that is like. It also removes the hierarchy of a team without offense.

continued →

WHAT THE ROADBLOCK LOOKS LIKE	WHAT THE TEAM'S RESPONSE SHOULD BE
ROADBLOCK: Personality Differences	
Teachers are human, and sometimes different personalities just don't mesh well together. Oftentimes, these are personal beliefs and individual ways of life.	Teams should focus strictly on honest data and the practices that help students perform best. As long as the data and collaboration are *always* focused on student learning instead of teacher teaching, then it should not matter whether teachers' personalities are compatible.
ROADBLOCK: Ego	
Inherently, teachers want to do a good job. This often means that their style or approach to teaching is very personal to the individual teacher. They believe what they are doing is best.	Too often, when teams focus on which teacher taught something the best, they place their focus on an individual teacher instead of the practices that the teacher used to see the students be successful. Changing their mindset from teacher success to student learning for *all* students will help pivot the conversation in a more positive and helpful direction for everyone involved. Isn't it equitable that *all* students receive the best education?
ROADBLOCK: Lack of Knowledge	
The saying, "You don't know what you don't know," often relates to teachers. Sometimes, teams look at the teacher who is struggling as dead weight or someone who cannot cut it.	Teams should look at the teacher who may be struggling as a great way to improve not only that teacher's practice but their own. Through constant reflection together as experienced or new teachers, the team will make their goals more specific and targeted while teaching the struggling teacher what they should be focusing on.
ROADBLOCK: Competition	
Because of high-stakes testing, teachers often look at each other as the competition. They do not want to share anything with their teammates because the teacher with the best test scores at the end of the year is the "winner."	This makes sharing best practices and honest data difficult for some teachers. Again, doesn't every student deserve an equitable education? When a team decides to shift their thinking to *all means all* instead of *all means "my students,"* true collaboration can begin and be productive.
ROADBLOCK: No One to Collaborate With	
Either a teacher is a singleton elective teacher or the school is a small school with one teacher per subject per grade.	When a teacher truly does not have people to collaborate with as a specific team, look around at who else is working on a goal similar to the teacher's. Are there different grade-level teachers teaching the same subject? Is there an arts and theater teacher who can collaborate? Look for other educators in either the same school or the same district who have the same goals in mind and can meet to better each other.

Figure 7.2: Roadblocks and team responses.

CELEBRATE TEAM SUCCESSES

Every professional needs to feel validated, appreciated, and understood for them to continue doing their job successfully. Here are some ideas to make collaboration fulfilling and beneficial for a teacher without costing any money.

- Celebrate a teacher's honesty. If a teacher struggles with a certain student or unit, celebrate that they feel comfortable enough to come to the team and ask for advice. That means that there is trust between the individual educators.

- Compliment each other's strengths when they are noticed.

- Be willing to share each other's students, whether it is for intervention or extension or a teacher simply needs a break from a student. Share the load.

- Be humble enough to say thank you.

- Write a note for a teacher on the team who does something admirable.

It is imperative that everyone in the whole school be committed to a specific purpose. However, it is just as vital that a team of teachers also be committed to each other, working together to achieve a common goal for their students.

TRY TO HEAD OFF CONFLICT

Occasional team conflict is inevitable even if a whole team is committed. Keep in mind that conflict comes in two forms: (1) healthy and (2) unhealthy. Healthy conflict may include differences of opinion on a team's practices, such as essential standards or proficiency. Healthy conflict is never a personal attack, and it keeps student learning as the focus. However, believing that seniority rules is unhealthy; it has nothing to do with students learning.

For a coach, it is critical to have a team's pulse and provide direction before conflict occurs, if possible. Help teams focus on engaging in inquiry and not taking feedback personally, creating norms to regulate healthy conflict, being aware of nonverbal communications, and being cognizant of each person's individuality (Bayewitz et al., 2020). After all, a team is easily composed of people of all walks of life: someone who's been teaching for thirty-five years and someone who's in the first year, extroverts and introverts, visual and kinesthetic learners, someone who grew up overseas and someone who grew up in the town where the school is located.

Communicate these items to your team but be ready to mediate if the need arises. If mediation is necessary, use consensus to move the team to action. For example, a coach can act as mediator. Sometimes that means coaching a team lead about how to manage a difficult team member; sometimes it means attending meetings to ask pertinent questions to help clarify the steps in the process; sometimes it means acting as the neutral party to conduct a vote. Whatever the situation, a coach can add that extra level of validation. Consensus does not mean 100 percent agreement. It merely means that all voices were heard, and the team's majority has decided what occurs going forward. According to Douglas Reeves and Richard DuFour (2016):

> **In a true PLC, collaborative teams of teachers use evidence of student learning as a basis for collective inquiry into instructional practice. The conversation moves beyond war stories and personal preferences to explore which practices are leading to superior results.**

You can address the team's collective skills by posing the questions in figure 7.3 or having the team members work through the questions without you present. Deeper learning experiences may include gallery walks and role play to foster adult learning tailored to each team.

Does the team have an agenda for each meeting that reflects the focus of the team's work?	Does the team meet regularly with a purpose?
Are the items on the agenda directly connected to the four critical questions of a PLC?	Does the team have a strategy to manage conflict?
Does the team have norms that are specific to the items the team struggles with?	Which strategies elicited the best results?
Are the norms referred to often and followed?	Are there different strategies for different learners (such as special education learners and high-achieving learners)?
Have all team members had the opportunity to voice their opinions and be heard?	Does the team consistently set and achieve student learning goals for each unit of instruction?

Figure 7.3: Question bank—Focused collaboration.

Reflect to Elicit Change

Reflection is the final key. After completing the supplied forms and having the suggested conversations, determine what work to celebrate. What are the next steps for the team? Once again, through carefully guided questions, a coach identifies strengths and areas in need of focus, and then determines what resources will help the team move forward in their work.

Figure 7.4 is an example team coaching inventory; complete this with your team.

		START	STOP	CONTINUE
	FOCUSED COLLABORATION	Meeting once a week during our common prep time	Taking comments personally (and instead be open to the idea that sometimes the suggestion is a better approach)	Growing and using the team's collective skills
SMART Goal		Create team norms that address the specific issues of our team, assign jobs for each team member regarding our meetings, and focus our meetings on the four critical questions of a PLC.		
Reflection		We're discovering that collaboration sometimes seems to be a challenge, but is necessary. We had to adjust and more clearly articulate the behaviors (our norms) that will make our collaboration efforts successful as we encountered challenges during the year. Using an agenda that had specific roles for each team member helped us be accountable to each other and kept us from slipping back into our old habit of only talking in the hall. We still talk in the hall to solve immediate problems, but our team meetings have meaning beyond griping and scheduling.		

Figure 7.4: Example of team coaching inventory.

Don't Miss This

Be aware of the following things while leading and coaching the journey.

- **Effective collaboration is a skill that leaders and coaches teach and model for teams:** Leaders need to create the necessary time for teachers to collaborate and also build a shared understanding of *why* teachers must collaborate and *how* they effectively collaborate through clearly articulating what the work of teams looks like. (Use the reproducible "What We Collaborate About," page 160.)

- **Collaboration is a team learning process:** Teams should frequently evaluate the strengths and areas to focus on as they work to improve their collective practices. Unit by unit, year after year, teams will gain a more sophisticated understanding of ways to utilize their strengths to ensure that *all* students learn the essential standards and skills for the course or grade level.

- **All teams are different:** Teams need different levels of support as they learn together and move forward in their collective work—just like students do in the classroom. When coaching a team, first recognize and validate its strengths. Following this, identify next steps or areas to focus on.

- **Monitor the work of teams:** Once leaders have provided the necessary time for teams to collaborate, they monitor the work of teams by asking evidence-based questions to assist the teams in their growth. Again, the evidence-based questions that leaders ask are not designed to micromanage. Instead, they guide leaders who are identifying a team's strengths and areas that could benefit from coaching.

What We Collaborate About

These questions help teams focus their discussions and collective actions during collaborative meetings at three different times during a unit of instruction: (1) planning the unit, (2) learning during the unit, and (3) reflecting on the unit. By providing this form to teams and teachers, administrators can help set team expectations. Team leaders can use this form to guide their discussions during collaboration by including specific questions on the agenda, and they can use it to know what kind of evidence to gather for administrators. Coaches can use this form as a checklist to provide data and feedback while observing team collaboration.

PLANNING THE UNIT	LEARNING DURING THE UNIT	REFLECTING ON THE UNIT
☐ Which essential standards and skills are part of this unit?	☐ Does our instruction meet or exceed the grade-level standards?	☐ Have we identified the students who still require extra time and support in a specific target?
☐ What will a student with mastery know and be able to do?	☐ Are we making learning progressions visible by sharing examples of various levels of work with our students?	☐ What is our team's plan for providing extra time and support for students who require it?
☐ Have we shared with students the learning targets and exemplars of mastery work?	☐ What are we learning from the formative feedback prompts we are asking students?	☐ According to our team formative assessment data, which strategies and practices were most effective?
☐ What critical vocabulary terms will students need to know during this unit?	☐ With data from our team formative assessments, have we determined the following?	☐ What did our team learn after teaching this unit?
☐ What formative feedback prompts will we ask during instruction?	→ Who has achieved mastery	☐ What successes can our team celebrate for this unit?
☐ Which team formative assessments will we use during this unit?	→ Who needs extra time and support	☐ Did we meet our team goal for this unit?
☐ When will we give the team formative assessments?	→ Which teaching strategies have been most effective	
☐ What strategies and practices have worked for this unit in the past?	→ Which questions or tasks students have struggled with	
☐ What is our team goal for this unit?	☐ How will we divide and provide students with extra time and support during the unit?	

Monitoring Collaboration

Use these questions to monitor a team's collaborative efforts. As team and school leaders ask the collaborative team each question, they look for specific evidence and identify strengths and areas of needed support. Leaders share the questions with the team at the beginning of each year so members know what they will have to respond to and they can prepare evidence.

Team:	Date:
ESSENTIAL STANDARDS AND SKILLS	**EVIDENCE**
Which essential standards have been **learned** (not only taught)?	
What evidence do you have that the **students learned** them?	
TARGETED ASSESSMENT	**EVIDENCE**
What are the names of **specific students** who have not mastered the essential standard or skill?	
What evidence do you have that you're providing **multiple opportunities** for the students to demonstrate mastery?	
EXTRA TIME AND SUPPORT	**EVIDENCE**
What evidence do you have that your team is providing **extra time and support** for students who require it?	
What evidence do you have that your team is **extending the learning** for those students who already know it?	
STRENGTHS AND CELEBRATIONS	**SUPPORT NEEDED**

Simplifying the Journey © 2024 Solution Tree Press • SolutionTree.com
Visit **go.SolutionTree.com/PLCbooks** to download this free reproducible.

Weekly Team Meeting Agenda

Team name:	Date:
Team leader:	Norm checker:
Documenter:	Timekeeper:

NORMS (REVIEW PRIOR TO EACH MEETING.)

Three minutes	**Celebrations**
Three minutes	**Business items**

Time:	Focus of meeting (Choose.)	Information and resources
	☐ Identify **essential standards**.	
	☐ Define **mastery for essential standard**.	
	☐ Plan **unit**.	
	☐ Develop **common formative assessments**.	
	☐ Review team formative assessment **data**.	
	☐ Identify the most effective **teaching strategies**.	
	☐ Design **team interventions**.	
	☐ Design **extensions**.	
	☐ **Other:**	

Five minutes	**Assignments for next meeting**

Assessing Our Reality

Directions: Your honest evaluation is critical! Please thoughtfully discuss the reality of your team in each of the target practices and behaviors. Use the following scale to rate your team in each target area. At the conclusion of each section, identify areas to celebrate and areas for your team to focus on.

3—This is very true of us! This is embedded in our beliefs and actions.

2—This is true of us some of the time. We need to be more consistent with this.

1—This is not true of us. This is definitely something we can work on.

RATING	THE COLLABORATIVE TEAM'S WORK
	Our team has identified shared norms that guide our collaborative teamwork and reviews the norms prior to each meeting.
	Our team consistently adheres to and honors our team norms and addresses violations in an immediate and respectful way.
	Our team respects and values the input of each team member as part of the team learning process.
	Our team collaboration is focused, productive, and a good use of our professional time.
	Our team uses our time to make decisions about learning with little conversational drift.
	Our team depends on the expertise of each member to ensure all students learn at high levels.

Celebrations:	Areas of Focus:

RATING	ESSENTIAL STANDARDS AND SKILLS
	Our team has identified the essential standards or skills for each unit of instruction.
	Our team has identified critical academic vocabulary that is shared prior to instruction.
	Our team has defined mastery for each essential standard or skill and shared it with students.
	Our team has agreed on how to best pace the instruction of the essential standards or skills.
	Our team shares examples of *approaching mastery* and *mastery* student work with the class.

Celebrations:	Areas of Focus:

RATING	TEAM FORMATIVE ASSESSMENT OR LEARNING FROM DATA
	Our team utilizes a variety of quick, targeted collaborative formative assessments during the unit to determine each student's progress toward the essential standards and skills.
	Our team provides opportunities for students to self-assess their progress and learning.
	Our team uses team formative assessment data to identify which teaching strategies elicit the best results with students.
	Our team analyzes team formative assessment data to determine which students need extra time.

Celebrations:	Areas of Focus:

RATING	EXTRA TIME AND SUPPORT
	Our team uses the results from the team formative assessments to determine which students need extra time and support in a targeted skill.
	Our team commits to using days as needed during the unit of instruction to provide extra time and support for students.
	Our team reteaches students who have not yet met mastery with the most effective strategies as identified in the collaborative formative assessment data.
	Our team provides extra time and support for students who have mastered the essential standard through extended learning opportunities.

Celebrations:	Areas of Focus:

RATING	

Celebrations:	Areas of Focus:

Final Thoughts

We, the authors, are proud to be educators. We know the majority of our colleagues entered this field to make a difference in the lives of students, working endless hours and doing their very best to meet the needs of every student who enters their classroom each day. The acknowledgment, not in the form of verbal and financial gratitude, often comes in the form of a thoughtfully crafted, occasionally misspelled handwritten note that simply says, "Thank you for being my teacher," or a big hug and tears from a student at the end of the year.

Simplifying the Journey is a guide to provide clarity for teachers and teams on their PLC journey with specific actions to help teachers, coaches, and leaders pay less attention to the pervasive educational noise and instead focus valuable time and effort on simplified actions that are proven to make a difference in student learning. Throughout this book, we have explored the power of simplification in a team's daily work. By implementing these efficient actions, you can replace unnecessary educational noise with simplified, effective practices that lead to increased student learning and greater gratification in your work.

There is no question that learning is messy. Our daily intentions are honorable, yet the messiness of our collective learning inevitably leads to a certain level of discomfort and dissonance. Working to ensure all students learn at high levels by engaging in effective collaborative work is tough! Keep in mind that as you engage in this work of learning together, that ever-present voice in your head (you know the one) will beckon you back to the comfortable, ineffective habits of old. We remind you that it's not referred to as a professional *perfection* community. The very essence of collaborative PLC work is as described in the word itself: a *community* of *professionals* who are *learning* together.

We can almost promise you won't get it right the first time. You will make mistakes, frustrations will emerge, and there most assuredly will be disagreements; all of these will *occasionally* be partners as you learn together. Commit to yourself, your team, and your school to passionately persist at learning together. As you do, we are confident you will realize the shared satisfaction that comes from overcoming mistakes and gaining clarity in the work that truly makes a difference in student learning and collective professional growth. Be persistent in creating the conditions for you and your colleagues to relentlessly pursue student learning and team growth. The adolescent authors of those thank-you notes you hold dear are the direct beneficiaries of your collective efforts.

In *Simplifying the Journey*, we have shared with you a process of six actions to help your team learn together and positively influence the students you serve.

1. **Identifying essential standards and skills that all students must know**

2. **Gaining shared clarity and clearly defining mastery**

3. **Creating student ownership through student self-assessment**

4. **Using formative assessment for feedback for teaching and learning**

5. **Learning together from team formative assessment data**

6. **Creating extra time and support to intervene and extend learning**

All is completed through frequent, intentional team collaboration that is focused on the six actions.

We humbly conclude with the heartfelt challenge left to each of us as educators by educational thought leader Richard DuFour (2015): "Will you act with a sense of urgency, as if the very lives of your students depend on your action, because in a very literal sense, more so than at any other time . . . , they do?" (p. 254).

We encourage you to embrace the practical strategies found in this book by replacing clutter and confusion with clarity and efficiency. Commit now to leverage the collective expertise of your colleagues as you learn together to collectively benefit *all* your students. Let the incredible weight of teaching in isolation be replaced by impactful, collaborative learning. We are wholeheartedly cheering for you as you begin your journey by replacing the incredible weight of teaching in isolation with a fresh mindset and renewed urgency to engage in and lead this important work of student and adult learning. We believe in you.

References and Resources

Aguilar, E. (2013). *The art of coaching: Effective strategies for school transformation.* San Francisco: Jossey-Bass.

Arizona Department of Education. (2018). *5.NF.B.6.* Accessed at https://k12standards.az.gov/content/5nfb6 on August 21, 2023.

Bailey, K., & Jakicic, C. (2023). *Common formative assessment: A toolkit for Professional Learning Communities at Work* (2nd ed.). Bloomington, IN: Solution Tree Press.

Bailey, K., Jakicic, C., & Spiller, J. (2014). *Collaborating for success with the Common Core: A toolkit for Professional Learning Communities at Work.* Bloomington, IN: Solution Tree Press.

Baldwin, M., & Mussweiler, T. (2018). The culture of social comparison. *Proceedings of the National Academy of Sciences of the United States of America, 115*(39), E9067–E9074. Accessed at www.pnas.org/doi/10.1073/pnas.1721555115 on June 17, 2023.

Bayewitz, M. D., Cunningham, S. A., Ianora, J. A., Jones, B., Nielsen, M., Remmert, W., et al. (2020). *Help your team: Overcoming common collaborative challenges in a PLC at Work.* Bloomington, IN: Solution Tree Press.

Brefi Group. (2014). *Covey's four quadrants for time management.* Accessed at www.crowe-associates.co.uk/wp-content/uploads/2013/10/Coveys-4-quadrants-Exercise.pdf on July 26, 2023.

Brown, B. (2018, October 15). *Clear is kind. Unclear is unkind.* Accessed at https://brenebrown.com/articles/2018/10/15/clear-is-kind-unclear-is-unkind on December 31, 2022.

Brown, T., & Ferriter, W. M. (2021). *You can learn! Building student ownership, motivation, and efficacy with the PLC at Work process.* Bloomington, IN: Solution Tree Press.

Buffum, A., & Mattos, M. (Eds.). (2015). *It's about time: Planning interventions and extensions in elementary school.* Bloomington, IN: Solution Tree Press.

Buffum, A., Mattos, M., & Malone, J. (2018). *Taking action: A handbook for RTI at Work.* Bloomington, IN: Solution Tree Press.

Coe, R., Rauch, C. J., Kime, S., & Singleton, D. (2020, June). *Great teaching toolkit: Evidence review.* Cambridge, England: Cambridge Assessment International Education.

Conzemius, A. E., & O'Neill, J. (2014). *The handbook for SMART school teams: Revitalizing best practices for collaboration* (2nd ed.). Bloomington, IN: Solution Tree Press.

DuFour, R. (n.d.). *The need for widely-dispersed leadership* [Video file]. Accessed at https://app.globalpd.com/search/content/NzU= on August 25, 2023.

DuFour, R. (2015). *In praise of American educators: And how they can become even better.* Bloomington, IN: Solution Tree Press.

DuFour, R., DuFour, R., Eaker, R., Many, T. W., & Mattos, M. (2016). *Learning by doing: A handbook for Professional Learning Communities at Work* (3rd ed.). Bloomington, IN: Solution Tree Press.

Eaker, R. (2020). *A summing up: Teaching and learning in effective schools and PLCs at Work.* Bloomington, IN: Solution Tree Press.

Evers-Gerdes, B. J., & Siegle, R. (2022, June 20). Six steps toward teacher retention and a long-lasting legacy [Blog post]. *Solution Tree Blog.* Accessed at www.solutiontree.com/blog/six-steps-toward-teacher-retention-and-a-long-lasting-legacy/#more-6849 on August 30, 2022.

Ferriter, W. M. (2016, April 19). New feedback activity: Unit analysis forms [Blog post]. *The Tempered Radical.* Accessed at https://blog.williamferriter.com/2016/04/19/new-feedback-activity-unit-analysis-forms on December 30, 2022.

Ferriter, W. M., & Cancellieri, P. J. (2017). *Creating a culture of feedback.* Bloomington, IN: Solution Tree Press.

Fisher, D., Frey, N., & Almarode, J. (2019). 5 questions PLCs should ask to promote equity. *The Learning Professional, 40*(5), 44–47. Accessed at https://learningforward.org/journal/resilient-leadership/5-questions-plcs-should-ask-to-promote-equity on April 17, 2023.

Gallagher, K. (2009). *Readicide: How schools are killing reading and what you can do about it.* Portland, ME: Stenhouse.

Glass, K. T. (2020). *Reading and writing instruction for fourth- and fifth-grade classrooms in a PLC at Work.* Bloomington, IN: Solution Tree Press.

Guskey, T. R. (2003). What makes professional development effective? *Phi Delta Kappan, 84*(10), 748–750. Accessed at https://journals.sagepub.com/doi/abs/10.1177/003172170308401007?journalCode=pdka on April 17, 2023.

Hannigan, J., Hannigan, J. D., Mattos, M., & Buffum, A. (2021). *Behavior solutions: Teaching academic and social skills through RTI at Work.* Bloomington, IN: Solution Tree Press.

Hattie, J. (2015, October 27). We aren't using assessments correctly. *Education Week.* Accessed at www.edweek.org/policy-politics/opinion-we-arent-using-assessments-correctly/2015/10 on September 26, 2022.

Hattie, J., & Zierer, K. (2018). *10 mindframes for visible learning: Teaching for success.* New York: Routledge.

Hoegh, J. K. (2020). *A handbook for developing and using proficiency scales in the classroom.* Bloomington, IN: Marzano Resources.

Knight, J. (2018). *The impact cycle: What instructional coaches should do to foster powerful improvements in teaching.* Thousand Oaks, CA: Corwin.

The Learning Pit. (2018, May 1). *Hattie: Collective efficacy* [Video file]. Accessed at https://vimeo. com/267382804 on December 30, 2022.

Lickona, T., & Davidson, M. (2005). *Smart & Good High Schools: Integrating excellence and ethics for success in school, work, and beyond.* Cortland, NY: Center for the 4th and 5th Rs.

Many, T. W., & Horrell, T. (2022). Prioritizing the standards using R.E.A.L. criteria. In T. W. Many, M. J. Maffoni, S. K. Sparks, & T. F. Thomas, *Energize your teams: Powerful tools for coaching collaborative teams in PLCs at Work* (pp. 97–99). Bloomington, IN: Solution Tree Press.

Many, T. W., Maffoni, M. J., Sparks, S. K., & Thomas, T. F. (2018). *Amplify your impact: Coaching collaborative teams in PLCs at Work.* Bloomington, IN: Solution Tree Press.

Marzano, R. J. (2017). *The new art and science of teaching.* Bloomington, IN: Solution Tree Press.

Massachusetts Department of Elementary and Secondary Education. (2017). *2017 curriculum framework for mathematics: Detailed revisions of 2010 standards for PK–12.* Malden, MA: Author. Accessed at www.doe.mass.edu/frameworks/math/2017-06revisions.pdf on August 2, 2022.

McMillan, J. H. (2014). *Classroom assessment: Principles and practice for effective standards-based instruction* (6th ed.). Boston: Pearson.

National Governors Association Center for Best Practices & Council of Chief State School Officers. (2010). *Common Core State Standards for English language arts and literacy in history/social studies, science, and technical subjects.* Washington, DC: Authors. Accessed at www.corestandards.org/ assets/CCSSI_ELA%20Standards.pdf on July 25, 2023.

Nebraska State Board of Education. (2017). *Nebraska's college and career ready standards for science.* Lincoln, NE: Author. Accessed at www.education.ne.gov/wp-content/uploads/2017/10/ Nebraska_Science_Standards_Final_10_23.pdf on August 2, 2022.

Next Generation Science Standards. (2013). *1-PS4-3 waves and their applications in technologies for information transfer.* Accessed at www.nextgenscience.org/pe/1-ps4-3-waves-and-their-applications-technologies-information-transfer on August 25, 2023.

O'Connor, K. (2007). The last frontier: Tackling the grading dilemma. In D. Reeves (Ed.), *Ahead of the curve: The power of assessment to transform teaching and learning* (pp. 127–145). Bloomington, IN: Solution Tree Press.

Pellegrino, J. W., & Hilton, M. L. (Eds.). (2012). *Education for life and work: Developing transferable knowledge and skills in the 21st century.* Washington, DC: National Academies Press.

Popham, W. J. (2013, January 9). Formative assessment's "advocatable moment." *Education Week, 32*(15), 29. Accessed at https://ew.edweek.org/nxtbooks/epe/ew_01092013/index.php#/p/28 on April 17, 2023.

Reeves, D., & DuFour, R. (2016). The futility of PLC lite. *Phi Delta Kappan, 97*(6), 69–71. Accessed at https://kappanonline.org/the-futility-of-plc-lite on July 7, 2023.

Richardson, J. W., Bathon, J., & McLeod, S. (2021). *Leadership for deeper learning: Facilitating school innovation and transformation.* New York: Routledge.

Stack, B. M., & Vander Els, J. G. (2018). *Breaking with tradition: The shift to competency-based learning in PLCs at Work.* Bloomington, IN: Solution Tree Press.

Siggins, K. (2020, March 5). The power of positive feedback. *Business and Industry Connection Magazine.* Accessed at www.bicmagazine.com/departments/hr/power-of-positive-feedback on July 27, 2023.

Stiggins, R. (2007). Assessment *for* learning: An essential foundation of productive instruction. In D. Reeves (Ed.), *Ahead of the curve: The power of assessment to transform teaching and learning* (pp. 59–76). Bloomington, IN: Solution Tree Press.

Stiggins, R., & Chappuis, J. (2005). Using student-involved classroom assessment to close achievement gaps. *Theory Into Practice, 44*(1), 11–18.

Utah State Office of Education. (2013). *Utah Core State Standards for English language arts and literacy in history/social studies, science, and technical subjects.* Salt Lake City, UT: Author. Accessed at www.schools.utah.gov/file/f087ed42-20cd-4c6a-8f25-0bd1091c6818 on July 25, 2023.

Waack, S. (2015, October 27). *Hattie ranking: 252 influences and effect sizes related to student achievement.* Accessed at https://visible-learning.org/hattie-ranking-influences-effect-sizes-learning-achievement on October 24, 2022.

Waack, S. (2018, March 7). *Collective teacher efficacy (CTE) according to John Hattie.* Accessed at https://visible-learning.org/2018/03/collective-teacher-efficacy-hattie on September 5, 2022.

Webb, N. L. (1997). *Criteria for alignment of expectations and assessments in mathematics and science education* (Research Monograph No. 6). Madison: University of Wisconsin–Madison, National Institute for Science Education.

Williams, K. (2022). *Ruthless equity: Disrupt the status quo and ensure learning for all students.* Wish in One Hand Press.

Woolf, N. (2020, February 10). *What research says about giving effective feedback to students.* Accessed at https://insidesel.com/2020/02/10/researchbrief-feedback on June 21, 2023.

Zapata, Y. P., & Brooks, R. (2017). *Adapting unstoppable learning.* Bloomington, IN: Solution Tree Press.

Index

A

agendas

  examples of, 43, 153–154

  and gaining shared clarity, 42

  and grade norming, 104

  and identifying essential standards and skills, 19

  reproducibles for, 29–31, 56, 164

  weekly team meetings, 152, 154

assessments. *See also* formative assessments; self-assessments

  assessing specific skills, 100–101

  coaching considerations for, 42

  end-of-unit assessments, 5, 6

  evaluating for validity, 101–102

  and identifying essential standards and skills, 16

  and reflection, 155

  verbs for determining instructional and assessment rigor, 102–103

B

Bathon, J., 6

Buckingham, M., 90

C

casual-observer strategy, 150

centers, 67, 68

clarifying and communicating the work. *See also* leading the work—specific actions of school and team leaders

  about, 7

  for creating extra time and support for learning, 130

  for encouraging student ownership through student self-assessment, 64

  for engaging in focused, productive collaboration, 148–149

  for gaining shared clarity and defining mastery, 36–38

  for identifying essential standards and skills, 14–15

for learning from formative data, 117

for utilizing formative assessments for feedback, 88–89

coaching the work—specific actions of learning coaches. *See also* planning and gathering evidence; reflecting to elicit change; scenarios for coaching the work

about, 7–9

for creating extra time and support for learning, 132–141

cyclical pattern for coaching, 7–8

for encouraging student ownership through student self-assessment, 65–83

for engaging in focused, productive collaboration, 151–159

examples of team coaching inventories, 27, 55, 83, 105, 126, 141, 159

for gaining shared clarity and defining mastery, 40–55

for identifying essential standards and skills, 17–26

for learning from formative data, 119–126

for supporting teachers as they learn together, 64

for utilizing formative assessments for feedback, 91–104

collaborative teams

development of, 149–150

and formative assessments, 89

and gaining shared clarity and defining mastery, 36

impact of, 147

monitoring the work of, 150

in PLCs, 158

in *Simplifying the Journey*, 2

and team formative assessment data, 115, 116, 117

collective skills, 140, 151, 152, 158

collective teacher efficacy, 120, 125, 136, 151

conflict/disagreements

trying to head off, 157–158

weekly team meetings and, 152, 154

Covey, S., 152

creating extra time and support for learning

about, 129

actions of *Simplifying the Journey*, 3, 4, 6

coaching the work for, 132–141

critical questions of a PLC and, 3

don't miss this, 141

examples of extra time and support data collection, 134–135, 138–139

leading the work for, 129–131

reproducibles for, 142–145

unit cycle of instruction and, 5

critical academic vocabulary, 37. *See also* shared clarity and mastery

cyclical pattern for coaching, 7–8

D

data. *See also* learning from formative data

data prompts for teams, 121–122

disaggregating the data, 133, 135

four data questions for teams, 118

defined mastery, 38. *See also* shared clarity and mastery

Depth of Knowledge (DOK), 37, 77–78, 102, 125

digital experiences to differentiate and individualize learning, 74

dine and shine, 17. *See also* validating and celebrating teams as they learn

DuFour, R., 158, 170

E

encouraging student ownership through student self-assessment. *See* student ownership through self-assessment

end-of-unit assessments, 5, 6. *See also* assessments

endurance, 16. *See also* identifying essential standards and skills

engaging in focused, productive collaboration. *See* focused collaboration

expectations

focused collaboration and, 147, 148

formative assessments and, 92, 100

gaining shared clarity and defining mastery
and, 42, 46, 48

graphic organizers and, 71

mastery and, 105

self-assessment and, 75, 83

extensions. *See also* creating extra time and
support for learning; interventions

and critical questions of a PLC, 2, 3

and culture, 141

deciding who will reteach and who will
extend, 135–137

example student choice menu with
different extensions, 71

and responding to students' learning
progress, 78

and response to intervention (RTI), 133

and schedules, 125

and student choice, 67, 70

F

feedback. *See also* utilizing formative
assessments for feedback

coaching the work and, 66

formative feedback prompts, 37

forms of, 88

timely, actionable feedback, 103–104

tips for providing validating feedback, 90

focused collaboration

about, 147

coaching the work for, 151–159

don't miss this, 159

example weekly team meeting agenda,
153–154

leading the work for, 148–151

reproducibles for, 160–167

formative assessments. *See also* assessments;
learning from formative data; utilizing
formative assessments for feedback

actions of *Simplifying the Journey*, 6

expectations and, 92, 100

formative feedback prompts, 37

prioritizing standards and, 130

unit cycle of instruction and, 5

front-row-seat-to-collaboration strategy, 150

G

gaining shared clarity and defining mastery.
See shared clarity and mastery

gaining shared clarity cards, 43, 44, 57

goals

example of goal setting, 74

self-assessment and, 78

SMART goals, 9

student choice and, 74

student ownership and, 67

three big ideas of a PLC and, 148

go-forth-and-collaborate strategy, 150

Goodall, A., 90

grade-level teams, 147

graphic organizers, 71, 73

H

Hattie, J., 77, 87

high-low comparisons, 71, 72

I

identifying essential standards and skills

about, 13–14

actions of *Simplifying the Journey*, 4, 6

coaching the work for, 17–26

critical questions of a PLC and, 2, 3

don't miss this, 27–28

example identifying the essential standards
and skills cards, 22, 23

examples of team essential standards guide,
25, 52, 53

leading the work for, 14–17

reproducibles for, 29–33

unit cycle of instruction and, 5

individualized education program (IEP), 36

individuals, use of term, 6

instruction

    instruction deficits, 123–124

    scenario for failing to separate the teacher from the instructional strategy, 116

    unit cycle of instruction, 5

inter-rater reliability, 104

interventions. *See also* creating extra time and support for learning; extensions

    and critical questions of a PLC, 132

    and culture, 141

    deciding who will reteach and who will extend, 135–137

    learning from formative data, 121, 123

    and prioritizing standards, 130

    and response to intervention (RTI), 123–124

    and schedules, 125

    and shared clarity and mastery, 38, 40

    and student choice, 67

introduction

    about *Simplifying the Journey*, 1–3

    actions of *Simplifying the Journey*, 3–6

    coaching the work—specific actions of learning coaches, 7–9

    don't miss this, 9

    leading the work—specific actions of school and team leaders, 6–7

    reproducibles for, 10–11

L

leading the work—specific actions of school and team leaders. *See also* clarifying and communicating the work; monitoring the work; supporting teachers as they learn together; validating and celebrating teams as they learn

    about, 6–7

    for creating extra time and support for learning, 129–131

    for encouraging student ownership through student self-assessment, 63–65

    for engaging in focused, productive collaboration, 148–151

    for gaining shared clarity and defining mastery, 36–40

    for identifying essential standards and skills, 14–17

    for learning from formative data, 117–119

    for utilizing formative assessments for feedback, 88–90

learning from formative data. *See also* formative assessments

    about, 115–116

    actions of *Simplifying the Journey*, 3, 4

    coaching the work for, 119–126

    critical questions of a PLC and, 3

    data prompts for teams, 121–122

    don't miss this, 127

    four data questions for teams, 118

    leading the work for, 117–119

    scenario for, 116

learning progressions

    making clear to students, 75–77

    responding to students' progress, 77–78

learning targets

    example of, 51

    gaining shared clarity and defining mastery and, 37

    unit cycle of instruction and, 5

learning together, 17. *See also* validating and celebrating teams as they learn

learning walks, 89

leverage, 16. *See also* identifying essential standards and skills

M

mastery. *See also* shared clarity and mastery

    common learning stages for teams in understanding mastery, 39

    defined mastery, 38

McLeod, S., 6

meetings

and creating extra time and support for learning, 130

creating meeting objectives, 155

and focused collaboration, 147, 149, 150, 152

and gaining shared clarity and defining mastery, 42, 44

and identifying essential standards and skills, 19, 24

and learning from formative data, 115, 123

weekly team meetings, 152, 154

monitoring the work. *See also* leading the work—specific actions of school and team leaders

about, 7

for creating extra time and support for learning, 130–131

for encouraging student ownership through student self-assessment, 64–65

for engaging in focused, productive collaboration, 150

for gaining shared clarity and defining mastery, 38–39

for identifying essential standards and skills, 16

for learning from formative data, 118–119

for utilizing formative assessments for feedback, 89–90

N

norms

creating, 148–149

example of, 148

identifying essential standards and skills and, 19

performing grade norming as a team, 104

reiterating team norms, 154

O

overwhelmed teachers, 66

P

pacing, 42

planning and gathering evidence. *See also* coaching the work—specific actions of learning coaches

about, 8

for creating extra time and support for learning, 133, 135–137, 140

for encouraging student ownership through student self-assessment, 67, 70–71, 74–78, 81–82

for engaging in focused, productive collaboration, 152, 154–155, 157–158

for gaining shared clarity and defining mastery, 42–43, 44, 45–48, 51, 54

for identifying essential standards and skills, 18–19, 22, 24, 26

for learning from formative data, 121–125

for utilizing formative assessments for feedback, 92, 100–104

Popham, W., 88

professional development, in-house professional learning, 17

professional learning communities (PLCs)

about, 169–170

four critical questions of, 2–3, 4, 76, 132, 154

Simplifying the Journey and, 1

three big ideas of, 8, 148

put-me-in-coach strategy, 150

Q

question banks

for creating extra time and support for learning, 140

for encouraging student ownership through student self-assessment, 82

for engaging in focused, productive collaboration, 158

for gaining shared clarity and defining mastery, 54

for identifying essential standards and skills, 26

for learning from formative data, 125–126

R

readiness, 15. *See also* identifying essential standards and skills

Reeves, D., 158

reflecting to elicit change. *See also* coaching the work—specific actions of learning coaches

    about, 8

    for creating extra time and support for learning, 140

    for encouraging student ownership through student self-assessment, 83

    for engaging in focused, productive collaboration, 158

    for gaining shared clarity and defining mastery, 54

    for identifying essential standards and skills, 26

    for learning from formative data, 126

    for utilizing formative assessments for feedback, 104

reproducibles for

    assessing our reality, 163–164

    extra time and support data collection—collaborative team, 144–145

    extra time and support data collection—individual teacher, 142–143

    gaining shared clarity, 61

    gaining shared clarity cards, 57

    gaining shared clarity—meeting agenda, 56

    identifying the essential standards and skills cards, 32

    identifying the essential standards—meeting agenda, 29–31

    monitoring collaboration, 161

    targeted unit plans, 106–113

    teacher team workshop—gaining shared clarity, 58–60

team coaching inventory, 10–11

team essential standards guide, 33

weekly team meeting agenda, 162

what we collaborate about, 160

resources, supporting teachers as they learn together, 64

response to intervention (RTI), 123–124

Richardson, J., 6

right work, focus on, 152

roadblocks, planning how to address, 155–156

rubrics

    example of, 76

    grade norming and, 104

    high-low comparisons and, 71

    involving self- and peer assessments and, 78, 81, 82

    learning from formative data and, 123

    learning progressions and, 75–76

    student involvement in evaluating learning and, 66

    utilizing formative assessments for feedback, 100

S

scenarios for coaching the work. *See also* coaching the work—specific actions of learning coaches

    about, 8

    for creating extra time and support for learning, 132–133

    for encouraging student ownership through student self-assessment, 65–66

    for engaging in focused, productive collaboration, 151–152

    for gaining shared clarity and defining mastery, 40–42

    for identifying essential standards and skills, 17–18

    for learning from formative data, 119–121

    for utilizing formative assessments for feedback, 91–92

school leaders. *See* leading the work—specific actions of school and team leaders

self-assessments. *See also* assessments; student ownership through self-assessment

    example of, 79, 80, 81

    involving self- and peer assessments, 78, 81–82

    planning and gathering evidence and, 75–78, 81–82

    responding to students' learning progress, 77–78

shared clarity and mastery

    about, 35–36

    actions of *Simplifying the Journey*, 3, 4

    coaching the work for, 40–54

    common learning stages for teams in understanding mastery, 39

    critical questions of a PLC and, 2, 3

    don't miss this, 55

    example learning targets for, 51

    example of, 49, 50

    example of meeting agenda for, 43

    example of teacher team workshop for, 45, 46, 47, 48

    example of team essential standards guide for, 52, 53

    gaining shared clarity cards, 43, 44, 57

    leading the work for, 36–40

    reproducibles for, 56–61

sharing students, 136, 137

singleton teachers

    disaggregating the data and, 133

    example of extra time and support data collection—individual teacher, 134–135

    extra time and support data collection—individual teacher, 142–143

    interventions and extensions and, 137

SMART goals, 8–9. *See also* goals

standards. *See also* identifying essential standards and skills

    example standards placed on a large table, 20

    example standards taped to a whiteboard, 21

    prioritizing, 130

sticky notes, 17. *See also* validating and celebrating teams as they learn

student choice/student choice menus, 67, 69, 71, 74

student deficits, 123–124

student involvement in evaluating learning, 66

student ownership through self-assessment

    about, 63

    actions of *Simplifying the Journey*, 3, 4

    coaching the work for, 65–83

    critical questions of a PLC and, 2, 3

    don't miss this, 83–84

    leading the work for, 63–65

student work descriptors, 123

supporting teachers as they learn together. *See also* leading the work—specific actions of school and team leaders

    about, 7

    for creating extra time and support for learning, 130

    for encouraging student ownership through student self-assessment, 64

    for engaging in focused, productive collaboration, 149–150

    for gaining shared clarity and defining mastery, 38

    for identifying essential standards and skills, 15–16

    for learning from formative data, 118

    for utilizing formative assessments for feedback, 89

T

targeted unit plans

    example of, 93–95, 96–99

    reproducibles for, 106–113

teachers, scenario for failing to separate the teacher from the instructional strategy, 116

team essential standards guide. *See also* identifying essential standards and skills

example of, 25, 52, 53

reproducibles for, 33

team formative assessment data. *See* learning from formative data

team leaders. *See* leading the work—specific actions of school and team leaders

time, 38, 64. *See also* creating extra time and support for learning

twice exceptional, 124

U

utilizing formative assessments for feedback. *See also* feedback; formative assessments

about, 87–88

actions of *Simplifying the Journey*, 3, 4

coaching the work for, 91–104

critical questions of a PLC and, 2, 3

don't miss this, 105

leading the work for, 88–90

reproducibles for, 106–113

V

validating and celebrating teams as they learn. *See also* leading the work—specific actions of school and team leaders

about, 7

celebrating team successes, 157

for creating extra time and support for learning, 131

for encouraging student ownership through student self-assessment, 65

for engaging in focused, productive collaboration, 151

for gaining shared clarity and defining mastery, 39–40

for identifying essential standards and skills, 17

for learning from formative data, 119

for utilizing formative assessments for feedback, 90

validation and celebration ideas, 131

vertical teams, 147

virtual teams, 147

voice, 27. *See also* identifying essential standards and skills

Leading Beyond Intention
Jeanne Spiller and Karen Power
School improvement starts with leaders. Take a deep dive into personal leadership skills and gain practical strategies for building capacity among your staff, growing your efficacy, and leading with intentionality each and every day.
BKF971

Powerful Guiding Coalitions
Bill Hall
Building a PLC is not a journey taken alone. That's where the guiding coalition comes in. With clear guidance, this book examines every aspect of how to create, develop, and sustain this essential team that will help champion and lead the change process.
BKF961

Energize Your Teams
Thomas W. Many, Michael J. Maffoni, Susan K. Sparks, and Tesha Ferriby Thomas
Help your teams get better faster. Written for busy school leaders, instructional coaches, and teacher leaders, this ultimate "grab-and-grow" guide details how to bridge the gap between learning and doing at every stage of the PLC journey.
BKG009

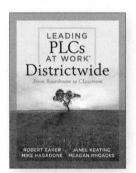

Leading PLCs at Work® Districtwide
Robert Eaker, Mike Hagadone, Janel Keating, and Meagan Rhoades
With this leadership resource as a guide, you will learn how to align the work of every PLC team within your district. Inspire professional learning communities to achieve continuous improvement and a guaranteed and viable curriculum for every student.
BKF942

The Big Book of Tools for Collaborative Teams in a PLC at Work®
William M. Ferriter
Organized around the four critical questions of PLC at Work, this resource provides collaborative teams with tools to become agents of positive change. Objectives are organized in an explicit structure to foster best practices in teaching and improve team learning outcomes.
BKF898

Solution Tree | Press

a division of
Solution Tree

Visit SolutionTree.com or call 800.733.6786 to order.